*Crisis management can be like
dancing with the tiger.*

*One must proceed carefully and
skillfully to avoid potential disaster.*

Dancing With The Tiger

The Art of Business Crisis Leadership

By Jim Truscott, OAM

www.businesscrisisleadership.com

eBook version available

Dancing With The Tiger: The Art of Business Crisis Leadership
by Jim Truscott

ISBN 978-0-615-65511-6

Visit the book website: www.businesscrisisleadership.com

Published by MissionMode Solutions Press
20 W. Kinzie St., Suite 1220, Chicago, IL 60654
Email: tigerbook@missionmode.com
Special quantity discounts are available. Contact the publisher for more information.

Printed in the USA

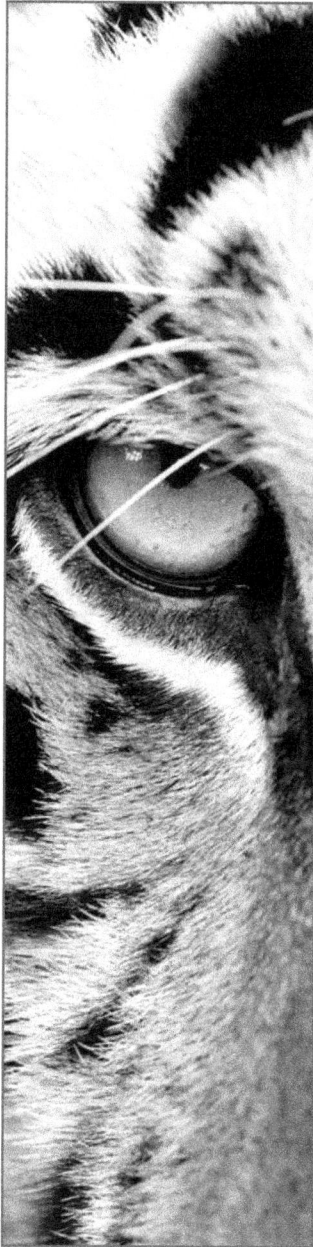

TRUSCOTT CrisisLeaders

Developing the capability to implement crisis strategies in the boardroom and deliver effective leadership under pressure.

Crisis practitioners operate from Australia, Brunei, China, Indonesia, India, Malaysia, Philippines, Papua New Guinea, Singapore, South Africa, Thailand and UAE.

Differentiators

Fundamental problem-solving and decision-making approach, enabling the capability to develop and implement plans and strategy under pressure.

Economic solutions based upon thin contingency plans and a first-principles approach, drawing upon professional response agency backgrounds, combined with commercial acumen.

Being able to manage risk more effectively and treat some risks as opportunities, through empowering subordinates, achieving management in depth, and sharing corporate experience.

Key Customers

Multi-national companies, listed companies and government in 20 countries across multiple sectors, including:

banking	insurance	water
broking	government	power
manufacturing	mining	construction
rail	aviation	oil & gas
maritime	energy	food
not for profit	fast-moving consumer goods	

Truscott Crisis Leaders

www.crisisleaders.com | jtruscott@crisisleaders.com

15 Kylie St, Wembley Downs, Perth, Australia, 6019

+61 8 9204 5141

VISION

Crisis
Leadership

Strategic
Management
of Emergencies

Emergency
Management

Emergency Response

When "dancing with the tiger," critical decisions are made under constant pressure. The game of business is played in the jungle and not on the playground.

Emergency Managers must patch holes in the fence—fix the problems. Their plans and actions must focus on getting "back to the past"—a solid status quo. Crisis leaders, however, must see beyond the holes in the fence. Their strategy will focus on getting "back to the future" and the opportunities that await.

This is vision, and it begins in the boardroom.

"Failure is not an option!"
–SAS saying

Table of Contents

About the Author

Jim Truscott, OAM has been a crisis practitioner for 30 years, cutting his teeth in the world of special operations and unconventional warfare with Australia's Special Air Service Regiment.

Military crisis resolution saw him intimately involved in multiple special situations in Africa, the Gulf and across Asia Pacific.

His foray into the corporate world in the last ten years has seen him cope with maggots in nursing homes, insider trading, fires on gas platforms in the South China Sea, misuse of market power, anchor drags on subsea pipelines in the Straits of Singapore, kidnappings in Sumatra, executives behaving badly, threats to gold mining in Kalimantan, the loss of financial processing centers and ships of shame off the Australian coast, amongst many other situations.

This is a guide for crisis champions who, like Jim, live a Jekyll-and-Hyde existence between wildly contrasting boardroom-based planning sessions and crisis operations-room emergencies on a daily basis.

When crisis strikes, its paralyzing effects on mind and body can be fixed by something simple:

- know what to do straight away
- know the first steps, and
- have the people and processes that take care of the early stages ready, rehearsed and prepared.

Then, as you have bought time up-front, paralysis is replaced by the practicality, improvisation and leadership that will bring you through the crisis.

The essence of "Dancing With The Tiger" is to buy you that time, and that essence comes from a person who is like the surgeon who has done fifty operations of exactly the kind you need. You would hire that surgeon for your ills; do the same with Jim Truscott for crisis leadership.

Inquiries should be directed to:

Truscott Crisis Leaders
jtruscott@crisisleaders.com
15 Kylie St, Wembley Downs, Perth, Australia, 6019
www.crisisleaders.com

About the Guide

The moral of the story is that information is just knowledge.

Experience is everything, and confidence comes from being able to apply that experience. Experience tells you what to do; confidence allows you to do it.

This guide is directed at the home of the crisis: organizations, businesses, companies, corporations and conglomerates for which crises are inevitable. It is primarily aimed at executives, directors and officers of organizations, who focus on corporate affairs, corporate governance, and compliance issues.

It also has application for readers interested in the management of failure and in raising the ethical bar.

This guide is unique as it contains strategies and concepts that are not found in existing breakthrough literature, but are in use by global crisis teams right now. It is written by a practitioner who has credibility across the private and public sectors, particularly amongst the top publicly-listed companies, as well as multinational companies.

It is the fruit of the mind of an inspirational and vastly experienced ex-Special Air Service officer, reflecting the approach of a Special Operative trapped in the body of a businessman.

In car racing, if you feel everything is under control, you are not going fast enough. In business, if you cannot solve problems, you are playing by the rules. It does not mean that you are going to crash; it is just that you are not going fast enough. For this reason, you have to take risks and be on the front of the wave to lead in business.

While there are many books in this subject area, some are dated by the numerous corporate governance practices that have come to fruition, drawing almost exclusively on examples with little relevance to the present scene in which social media and the cloud prevails.

As such, it is a guide to the application of current corporate governance measures, some being imposed by regulators and others being adopted voluntarily by organizations.

How to Use This Guide

It is a personal "pocket book" for crisis leaders. It can be used as a crisis plan if you do not have a crisis plan. Like an oversize wallet card, it captures hard and practical leadership experience.

The guide embodies pure leadership principles without decorative testimonials, which cannot be applied in the heat of the moment.

Acknowledgements

I am indebted to the following people in the production of this book:

Colette Truscott, Cathy McCullagh, Robert Kilsby, Matthew Rosser, Mark Ryan, David Borrill, Jack Hayes, Marc Preston and Wayne Blankenbeckler of MissionMode.

> *Rome may not have been built in a day,*
> *but it could certainly be destroyed in one.*

§

Dancing With The Tiger

*The Art of Business
Crisis Leadership*

CHAPTER 1

Crisis Governance

Navigating a Jungle of Confusion

The game of business is played in the jungle, not on the playground, and crisis management can be like dancing with the tiger—one must proceed carefully and skillfully to avoid potential disaster. Therefore, the rules of the jungle prevail when sidestepping the business snakes and climbing the business ladders.

The word "crisis" comes from the Greek word *krino*, to decide. It means a turning-point, especially of disease or a moment of danger or suspense in politics and commerce.

There is a vast and confusing array of colorful terminology used by the public and private sectors and within organizations to describe "crises" in all of its forms. This variance can be meaningless without the context for which these terms were designed.

Some organizations, for example, reduce their overall system of crisis and emergency management to the commonplace with terms such as disaster or incident management. Yet, there is nothing commonplace in the management of a true catastrophe.

Crises can range from national and international political events—often involving brinksmanship and psychological activities—to the personal catastrophe that occurs when an individual loses their job.

Whatever terminology is used, crisis governance is discussing the un-discussible and thinking the unthinkable. It is an acceptance that crises are part of business, requiring the converging of all styles of management. The better companies have moved from emergency response to crisis anticipation in the journey towards resilience.

The evolving business environment is moving from shareholder dominance to stakeholder dominance, from financial performance to triple bottom-line accounting, from an operational focus to a strategic focus, from simple compliance to balanced conformance and performance, and from financial risk to enterprise-wide non-financial aspects.

With relentless pressure to compete, perform globally, constantly enhance earnings, increase governance transparency, and have a broader societal role, the best companies are adopting crisis leadership as mainstream management.

The Evolving Business Environment

Shareholder dominance	Stakeholder dominance
Financial performance	Triple bottom line accounting
Operational focus	Strategic focus
Compliance	Balanced conformance and performance
Financial risk	Enterprise-wide non-financial aspects

Crises and Their Incubation

> *"Next week there can't be any crisis.*
> *My schedule is already full."*
> *- Henry Kissinger*

Crises occur when there is major interruption to business, often involving overwhelming debt or serious damage to reputation. All organizations have to identify their own crisis threshold. This threshold represents any turning point which falls outside normal business contingency and emergency response arrangements.

The word "crisis" can, however, be used in many other ways and be accompanied by a vast range of widely differing meanings. The expression "crisis of confidence" is often used by traditional and social media to describe the incubation of a true crisis, and the media's penchant to use the word crisis, can sometimes lead to media-induced crises.

Organizations prone to crises are generally characterized by a loss of corporate memory, fuzzy lines of responsibility, a resistance to learning, poor internal organization, and limited communication skills.

> *About half of all crises affect profits.*

It is a fact that the price exacted by public outrage, political pressure, shareholders, stock markets, and regulatory controls in the wake of crises far exceeds the costs of any operational response. About half of all crises interfere with business and affect profits; 70% of situations escalate.

Studies of corporate collapses and major disasters indicate that all organizations incubate crises, and that these situations simply require either an internal or an external trigger to be initiated. The threat is often internal rather than external, and the trigger may be totally unexpected, such as:

- government investigation, Director's liability, or legal action
- a hostile takeover
- loss of a significant supplier or customer
- strikes, redundancies and executive succession
- information loss, security breach, technology failure and terrorist activity
- reputation attacks, rumors, and media leaks
- bad debts and increases in insurance premiums

Ignorance gets organizations into trouble and arrogance keeps them there.

Will the Organization Pay You for Your Management or Leadership in a Crisis?

Managers are not paid for the routine work they do today, but rather for what they might have to do in the extraordinary circumstance that is tomorrow. This is the only rationale behind shareholder investment in what is essentially the unknown, and it is key to corporate survival.

People imagine the past and remember the future.

Crisis leaders are big-picture people who use power and passion to turn the camera on in peoples' minds. The art of crisis leadership is the ability not only to contain the problem when it occurs but also to take the organization past any advantage line and then transform the organization post-crisis.

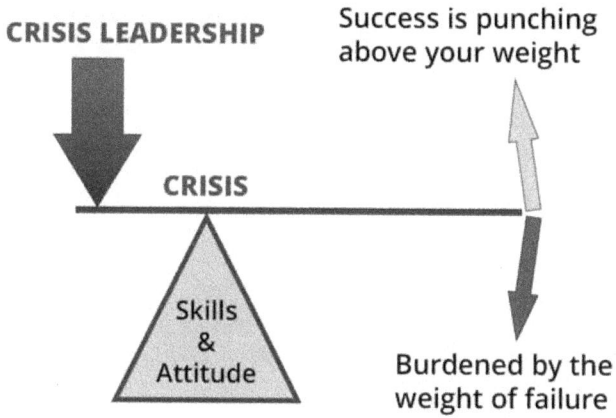

CRISIS LEADERSHIP

Success is punching above your weight

CRISIS

Skills
&
Attitude

Burdened by the weight of failure

Leadership in crisis is beyond command-and-control.

Competence in lower-order emergency management is simply a form of survival which seeks to return aberrant situations to normal. Crisis preparation is merely emergency management thinking, and traditional crisis management is just a form of insurance.

Hence, raw leadership is the best preparation for crises, as its 'back to the future' thinking will set an organization free through bold, creative second- and third-stage thought.

Traditional crisis management is just a form of insurance.

CHAPTER 2

Controlling and Coming Out of Crisis

Line Management

Organizational Unit

Organizational Unit

Organizational Unit

Organizational Unit

Crisis Team

Crisis Leadership

Transitioning from Line Management to Crisis Leadership

Transitioning from Line Management to Crisis Leadership

Crisis leadership occurs when day-to-day vertical line management transitions into horizontal team management. The move from vertical to horizontal management is necessary when organizations face the loss of normal management control, often as a result of having to deal with multiple stakeholders simultaneously.

| *Crisis leadership is a rapier-like tool.*

The challenge is often the speed of transition from vertical to horizontal, or from a reactive to a proactive management style.

In situations when line management is overwhelmed, there is no other successful approach. Crisis leadership may be necessary in order to regain control of an organization's reputation, ensure an organization's continuity, address overwhelming liabilities, or any combination of these issues.

Crisis leadership is the normal modus operandi of political cabinets, the military, and some dynamic organizations where it competes with line management for center stage. In these organizations, crisis leadership is the rapier-like tool that generates incredible business tempo and provides a strategic reserve in the face of risk.

The transition from line management to crisis leadership is achieved by:

- Activating the crisis team, call center, other crisis management technology, and business support teams as a default.
- Using physical and virtual team sessions, time-outs and updates to establish and check the facts.
- Brainstorming and prioritizing the key crisis issues concerning reputation, business continuity, and liability.
- Developing courses of action for regaining control and seizing business advantage.
- Implementing crisis strategy to regain a commercial position.

The Recognition of Crises and Lurking Crisis Situations

Triggers and Event Recognition

In an event-generated crisis, line managers will report a problem and begin to consider solutions. It is vital that crisis plans nominate a member of the organization who has the authority to declare a crisis.

This "no blame", or "Code Red", approach is particularly crucial in an organization with a culture that does not permit or expect staff to take charge. If the crisis does not originate through an internal trigger, recognition or notification may come externally from a regulator or competitor.

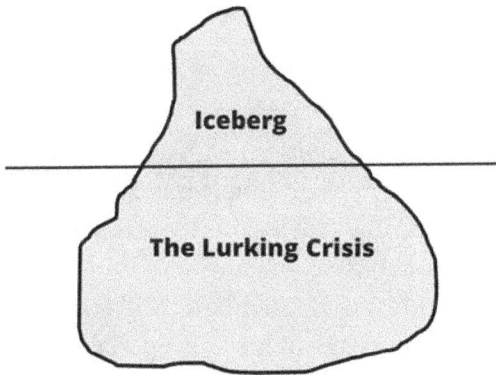

How to prepare for something that you do not know is going to happen?

The crisis leader may choose to use activation thresholds, commonly found in plans, to determine whether the situation they confront is a crisis or the undercurrent of a crisis situation—often referred to as a lurking, creeping or slow-burn crisis. Thresholds are based upon risk consequences, threat levels, media attention, business continuity processes, and involvement of stakeholders.

Some situations may lead to the organization assuming crisis mode, even though a formal state of crisis has not been declared. Crisis monitoring is managing special situations in periods of volatility, or in dealing with the slow burning or creeping crisis.

The Notification of Crises and the Use of Business Support Teams

Alternative Leadership and a Culture of Deputies

Irrespective of the origin of the crisis, whether internal or external, a manager should formally declare a crisis situation. A declaration enforces the change in management style at all levels, or, as a minimum, within the affected area.

Once a crisis is declared, the crisis leader will make contact with team members or task a personal assistant with assembling other managers. This notification process appears simple but is often characterized by a period of confusion during which crisis leaders and their own support teams assemble and establish contact with one another. Communications and HR support teams are standard in all sectors, and Investor and Government Relations teams are appropriate to others.

Crises are typically triggered outside of business hours or when team members are absent. This complicates an already chaotic situation, since there is a requirement to contact deputies or alternates.

As part of the planning process, team members should have identified a horizontal alternate, vertical deputy, or support team member to provide assistance during the crisis.

Crises also feature periods of inactivity as the site itself or the affected business unit bears the brunt of initial inquiries. During these periods, the team will strive to collect and process all available information.

Consider the use of technology here when speed and accuracy are of the essence, and changing the mind-set of individuals from vertical to horizontal working is crucial. Adopt a solution that works with the culture of the organization and the players involved.

Crisis management tools can focus teams into the right behaviors. Bear in mind, though, that different groups within an organization have different information needs and technology skills.

Activating the Crisis Response

The crisis response process is followed once a crisis has been declared or its potential has been recognized. Given the comprehensive nature of the activation process, it may take some time to complete it.

Once team members have been notified, they should redirect their office phones to the call center in order to ensure information flows at all times.

Strategic teams need quiet situation or breakaway rooms that are separate from the operations room. The crisis operations room is focused on managing any underlying event and thus is unsuitable as a location for brainstorming sessions and strategy formulation.

Teams should be prepared to meet at an alternate site, or even virtually (using conference bridges and virtual crisis operations rooms in the cloud), in the event that the normal building is not available.

It is normal practice to meet with business partners or government representatives in a venue specifically designated for that purpose. Meetings with partners and regulatory authorities should not be co-located with crisis team planning sessions, as they require a separate and permanent facility.

The crisis leader may decide to conduct a combined briefing of all teams, including staff, during the activation process. Such a decision will depend upon the personal style of the leader, who may want to brief the team, the call center, communications and HR support teams in a combined forum to ensure the accurate transfer of releasable information.

Should sensitive issues such as redundancy arise, a selective and private briefing of employees in one or more groups may also be required. Personnel issues may achieve an unwelcome prominence should the future of the organization itself be threatened.

Issues of a sensitive nature, such as employees' personal circumstances, should always be dealt with personally by the crisis leader. Employees can be an organization's best ambassadors during a crisis. If they are well-briefed with releasable information, they can be powerful and effective representatives.

Since staff members may be vulnerable to ambush by strategically-placed traditional and citizen journalists, they should not have to face the media in a confrontational situation or be used for traditional media interviews.

Nevertheless, employees remain among the organization's most effective means for disseminating messages in the public domain and through social media.

The Crisis Team

The crisis team is a tailored group of senior executives, managers, and staff within an organization that convenes to control or contain the crisis. In short, the best brains are put to the best use at the helm.

Crisis plans describe the composition of the team, the facilities it will use, and the locations at which it will meet. The plan should nominate a default team manning, but the crisis leader may select the most appropriate members and customize its composition.

Teams are always customized with the best intellectual effort possible to develop and implement crisis strategy. So, in this respect, any plan is only a guide.

Critical components of a crisis team

The deputy leader or process checker is a critical team member who coordinates information flow between the call center and all support teams. It may take several hours for the whole organization to begin working effectively, and teams must make allowances for this delay.

The deputy leader will face considerable challenges, despite the presence of well-documented procedures, as they invariably have to be adapted on short notice.

Teams must be very disciplined in their key actions to control crises and resume vertical line management. Crisis leaders must initially establish and check the facts to identify stakeholders and the relevant issues. Only then can they develop and implement strategies to regain control.

These actions are iterative, and remain incomplete until an effective strategy is actually implemented with stakeholders. Crisis leaders, who complete these actions but lack decisive leadership or cannot clearly articulate or implement a strategy, may never recover.

Also, crisis leaders often experience a strong urge to reach into their organizations to provide tactical advice. It is called leadership compression and it can be a deadly sin during a crisis.

This detailed focus on life, property, or environment tasks may be critical from time to time. The key, however, is to provide strategic direction in terms of business continuity, reputation and liability concerns.

Office Rhythm – Time & Team Discipline

> *Information is the key resource, truth is the primary value, and time is the greatest enemy.*

The crisis team's key actions must be instinctive and completed under pressure in a focused manner through the use of team sessions, time-outs, and updates. Disciplined workflow and process checks are vital.

Teams generally have fewer than 24 hours to devise or implement initial crisis strategy. So, managing time through team discipline is crucial, as winning time will always be the key to success. Thus, crisis leaders should make liberal use of the 'do it, dump it or delegate it' approach by scheduling team sessions as and when required.

Team Session

12

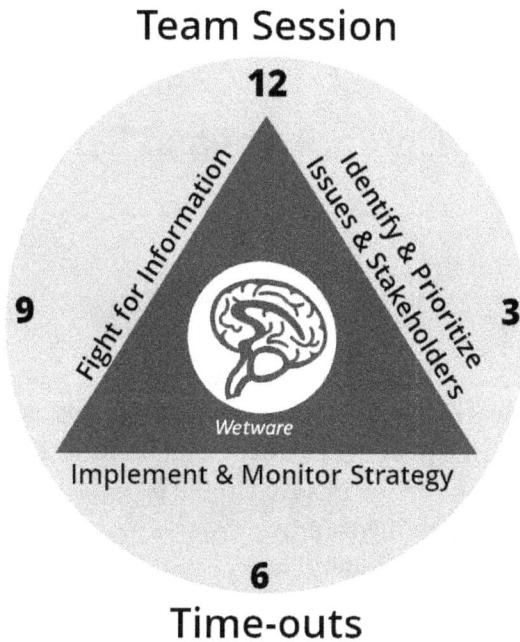

Fight for Information

Identify & Prioritize Issues & Stakeholders

Wetware

9

3

Implement & Monitor Strategy

6

Time-outs

Developing and implementing strategy in teams under pressure

A checklist as an element of a crisis plan can act as a useful aid in assisting crisis leaders to think and win time. Typically, however, many members and teams become mesmerized by procedures, manuals and plans during the process of developing and implementing strategy under pressure.

Checklists are an aid to management, but not necessarily to leadership. Checklists maybe used by team members to achieve non-wasted time, but crisis leaders should be circumspect in their use.

The process of dealing with multiple stakeholders simultaneously can be quite straightforward, given the correct approach. This approach ideally involves a succession of team sessions and time-outs within the deadlines imposed by traditional and social media, competitors, regulators or other key stakeholders.

Achieving Crisis Cadence and Setting Deadlines

Cut once; cut deep.

The crisis leader constantly must be mindful of approaching deadlines, particularly when a joint update may be required with other business support teams that may be involved in the process. Understanding deadlines for different media provides a useful insight, as time is also the traditional media's greatest enemy.

Crisis leaders should recognize that:

- Team sessions may typically last 30-40 minutes, and time-outs may be 20-30 minutes long.
- It's surprising how long it takes to make two or three telephone calls. This level of team activity is structured very much around the personal style of the crisis leader.
- Time-outs may become longer once teams are implementing strategy, as this requires team members to work closely with other managers and staff and to make contact with key stakeholders.

It should be noted that time-outs acquire a completely different meaning for emergency managers, who have an operations room mentality, as opposed to a situation or strategy-room mentality. Thus, emergency managers rarely leave their operations room unmanned.

A time-out for these managers is not an individual activity outside the room; rather, it is a team activity that's insulated from outside interference while the group constructs or amends a plan.

Updating the Crisis Team

"The situation, as I understand it, is this..."

Follow-up for team time-outs, updates, or executive recaps become necessarily crucial so as to reaffirm strategic focus. To do this, many crisis leaders will use a simple whiteboard to record updates and the reaffirmed focus.

Sharing this information across groups and locations can be a challenge, so investigate the use of cloud technology that can help, not hinder, the response.

Focus is determined by the scale and consequences of the crisis. One of the biggest challenges is making the transition from a reactive mode back to a proactive mode in the shortest possible timeframe.

When the crisis leader has an update, particularly if team members have been out of the room during a time out, they should:

- Commence with a very short summary of the situation, as they understand it.

- Call for any additional information that team members may have obtained during the time-out. This contribution by other team members should retain its factual focus, rather than becoming a general discussion.

- Outline or restate the team's focus and continue the team session.

The update process should take no more than five minutes, and some teams will find it necessary to document this update process in the interests of team discipline.

Fighting for Information

Fact-finding and fact-checking are continuous processes and must be very disciplined actions early on in a crisis—particularly since the team at that stage may not be complete.

One of the principles of crisis leadership is that facts are all-important. Nothing can be publicly released until the underlying facts are checked and verified by a number of independent sources.

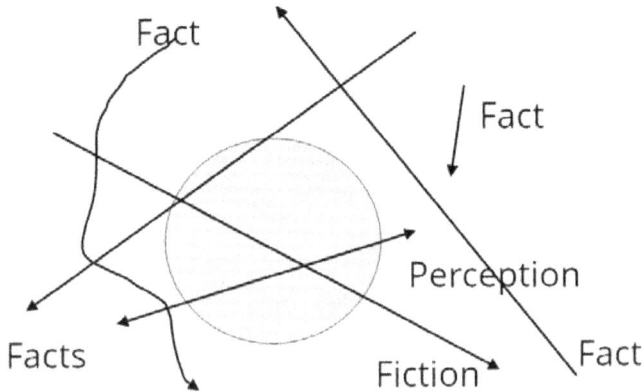

Finding and checking the facts is the hallmark of crisis management

Crises are typically confusing situations characterized by rumors, half-truths, and misleading information. Any recovery or management strategy must be grounded in the bedrock of fact.

Team members identify their information requirements for developing a crisis strategy. As time is of the essence, and as the team will be working with incomplete information, access to the latest updates is vital in the search for additional facts from stakeholders.

Key stakeholders may include the interested and the influential, such as:

- Affected and uninvolved employees, next of kin, or nominated emergency contacts
- Board members and legal advisers
- Existing and potential customers and suppliers
- Shareholders, financial analysts, bankers, and insurers
- Affected and interested third parties, such as unions, the local community, academia, and issue-motivated groups
- Government and statutory authorities
- Traditional and social media

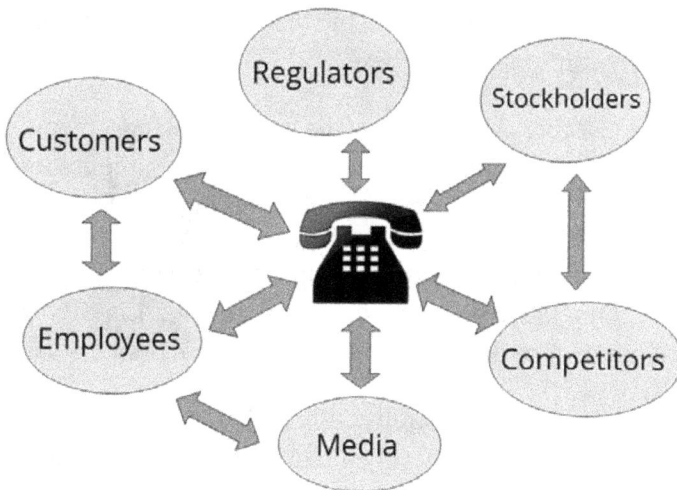

Identify and engage all involved stakeholders

Crisis plans must include a directory of key contacts to facilitate rapid communication with relevant stakeholders. Some teams also appoint a scribe, a team member separate to the log-keeper, to visually display facts.

As fact-finding progresses, the Corporate Affairs member should automatically commence compiling likely stakeholder questions and answers (Q&A). This tool is an excellent method of concurrently developing and articulating strategy.

Identifying and Prioritizing Crisis Issues

"Delete expectations, focus on possibilities."
– Ross Bentley, Race Driver Coach

With whatever facts are available, teams must initiate their strategy formulation with a comprehensive brainstorming of the early key issues. These issues will invariably relate to image, liability, and operability, or any combination of these.

While team members will consider the strategic management of life, property, and environment, it is business continuity, reputation and liability that ultimately will govern their thinking.

Tracking linkages between issues is important, particularly those that may impact on relative priorities for developing a crisis strategy or when dealing with multiple stakeholders on more than one issue.

Crisis strategy priorities generally will be obvious, although there will be an occasional equal between issues of reputation and business continuity.

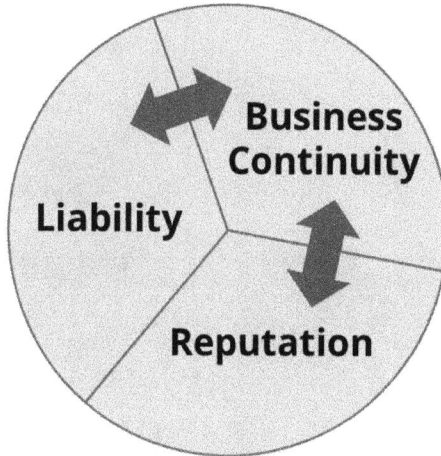

Identify and prioritize the business issues at stake

Developing Crisis Strategies

> *"Nothing is more dangerous than an idea when it's the only one you have."* – Emile Chartier

The English word strategy derives from the Greek word *strategos*, which means the art of the general. Crisis strategy is similar to running from a tiger; one need not run faster than the tiger, just faster than the next person. Thus, the team devises crisis strategy based upon:

- business experience
- an assessment of those factors that remain under the control of the organization
- any business plans that may be applicable

Normal business strategy generally involves some aspect of cost leadership or differentiation of product through innovation and service.

Cost Leadership

Plan

Ploy

Perspective

Differentiation of Product

Pattern

Process

Develop strategies, branches and sequels

Gaining control and creating opportunity: the essence of crisis strategy.

Crisis strategy, on the other hand, may take the form of a plan, ploy, pattern, process or perspective. Crisis strategy could comprise a:

- **Plan** - a contingency plan, which may already have been prepared or considered
- **Ploy** - outmaneuvering through psychological or physical actions
- **Pattern** - a pattern of consistent behavior
- **Position** - seeking advantage or exceeding expectations by going beyond the typical to afford a unique point of advantage
- **Perspective** - a perception shared by a group

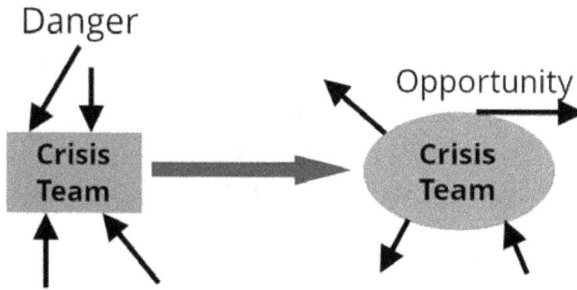

Respond to risk and seize any opportunities

Successful crisis strategies are usually those that seize business advantage. Thus, gaining control and creating opportunity are the very essence of crisis strategy.

If strategic options are not readily apparent, then parallel thinking quickly can harness the widest possible courses of action to overcome argument and individual egos within the members of a team working under pressure. This Edward de Bono technique for producing ideas and solutions beyond the obvious includes:

- **White** thinking: querying available, or missing, information
- **Red** thinking: intuition and emotion
- **Black** thinking: caution and risk
- **Yellow** thinking: making it work
- **Green** thinking: ideal for crises because it sees opportunity rather than danger, and seeks to use the crisis to transform the organization
- **Blue** thinking: process control

Teams can use a combination of these styles of thinking, or, depending on the issue, use a particular style such as red thinking to generate emotive thinking about strategy.

"Strategy is a system of makeshifts. It is more than a science. It is bringing knowledge to bear on practical life, the further elaboration of an original guiding idea under constantly changing circumstances. It is the art of acting under the pressure of the most demanding conditions.

That is why general principles, rules derived from them, and systems based on these rules cannot possibly have any value for strategy."

– Helmuth von Motlke,
Prussian Chief of the General Staff

Articulating and Implementing Crisis Strategy

"We see it happening this way."
Purpose, method and end state.

Strategy identification is ideally suited to the use of a catch phrase as the label for a chosen strategy. This could be "early admission," "do nothing," "hope," or an "attack" catch phrase. This labeling ensures ease of articulation and comparison with other courses of action.

Articulating and implementing crisis strategy is truly managing on the edge of darkness, with the caveat that no one tactic or trick constitutes crisis strategy.

Rather, an effective crisis strategy is the totality of the way in which an organization works to control the crisis and regain its commercial position.

In order to implement its strategy with stakeholders, an organization will use its:

- structure
- systems
- skills
- style
- staff
- shared values

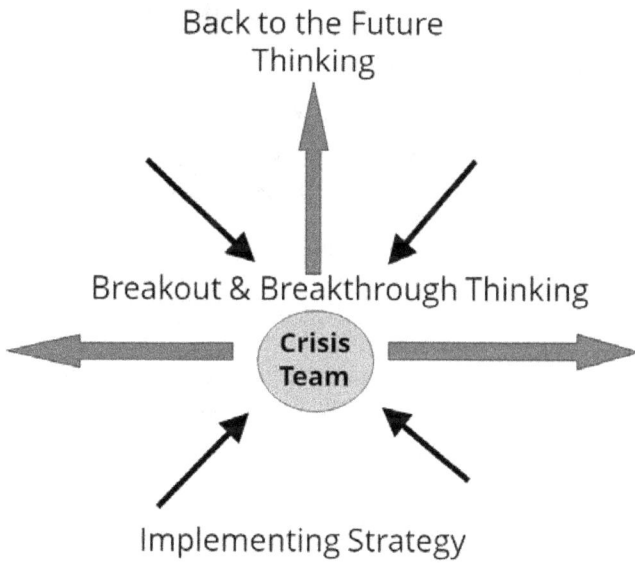

Implement strategy by direct contact with stakeholders

Implementing Business Continuity Strategy

Issues can be esoteric and crises pivot on the unknown, making crisis leaders explorers of Business Continuity.

Strategies to resume or transform business may be subject to regulatory controls and internal investigations. There may be many branches and sequels best suited to the management of staff, customers, and other key stakeholders in order to regain the organization's commercial position. Such strategies include:

- Industrial Relations strategies – opening dialogue, constructing an offer, resuming negotiations, or reaching an agreement.

- Sudden market shift strategies – locating the problem and developing the ability to adjust.

- Cash strategies – taking control to stem a cash hemorrhage, to raise new cash, re-establish credibility, or show a profit.

- Hostile takeover strategies – repelling or exhausting the attacker, considering the offer, informing the public, invoking protection, or eliminating the attraction.

- Regulation and deregulation strategies – exploiting the inevitable, co-opting the powerbrokers, implementing vigorous change, or preparing for tomorrow.

Some crises may simply require the application of a prepared business continuity plan. Other outage strategies could seek to eliminate the threat, focus on interim operations or deferred resumption, or even discontinuing the line of business.

Implementing Financial and Legal Liability Strategies

Liability strategies will detail the organization's position on legal relationships with stakeholders, outline how insurance can be exploited, and suggest guidelines for compensation as appropriate.

Despite the fact that most insurers require organizations to actively manage their risks, insurance:

- pay-outs will inevitably remain slow, and reputation per-se cannot be insured as a commodity.
- is generally not a cheap option due to the negative influence of large claims over environmental and product liability losses.
- does not usually recoup the full amount lost.
- plans do not commonly include open-ended coverage, which is no longer widely available.

50% of companies that lack adequate business interruption insurance do not survive disasters. Deductible clauses in policies also can make insurance less useful. Deductibles may be time-based, such as the first week, or a financial amount.

In either case, business continuity plans have to cover the gap. If you have faith in your plan, you can elect a bigger deductible and only cover extreme events.

You need simple tools to achieve rapid resolution on claims. Avoid adversarial settlements by planning how the insurance company may respond with the finances required in the days and weeks following a disaster.

A formula for settlement should be established in advance with processes and templates in plans for gathering claims data. These actions lead to swifter settlement, as complex scenarios can take several years.

Include insurance procedures in plans to collect claims information and keep the insurer updated. The location and accessibility of the plan is important in assessing its likely effectiveness. Testing and improving plans is critical to gaining insurer confidence, as insurers find that plans are often not tested or kept up-to-date.

Lawyers can often make repeated calls for criminal charges to be laid against organizations or individuals, or for generous, flat-rate payments to be made to all victims regardless of the merits of each claim. Lawyers can also urge a strategy of identifying and approaching political figures to represent the cause of the victims of a disaster with a view toward exploiting the resultant publicity.

Following a crisis in which there have been injuries, teams may need to be less concerned about claims for damages, and more concerned about potential criminal charges and how a criminal investigation should be handled.

If the organization is at fault, by far the best strategy is to accept a degree of blame and commence work on an effective mechanism for management of the ensuing consequences.

In circumstances that may give rise to compensation and—if reputation is the primary issue—then interim payments can be made to both mollify plaintiffs and buy valuable planning time. The best policy often involves an admission of liability sooner, rather than later.

Implementing Reputation Strategy

Reputation = Behavior + Communication

Crisis leadership involves much more than handling the media. However, it should be recognized that, as a stakeholder, both traditional and social media can play the single biggest role.

Gaining control of the media agenda early in a crisis prevents speculation. Taking charge of messaging is an effective means of regaining the initiative and infiltrating the stakeholders' decision loops.

The task of monitoring the media is beyond the capacity of one person to perform effectively. The designated Corporate Affairs member is also a crucial contributor to the team's overall strategy development and cannot be in two places at once.

Ideally, a Communications Support Team should be formed to analyze the media and assist in the dissemination of the organization's Single Overriding Communications Objective (SOCO), also known as the key message.

SOCO is simply the message that an organization wishes to convey. It will be a product of much debate, as the message heard by the stakeholder must be that of the organization's spokesperson and not that of a media observer.

If the public is confident that the organization is in control of media coverage, then, from the public's perspective, the possibility of an emergent crisis diminishes. With this in mind, the communications support team must:

- Analyze all traditional and social media.
- Formulate the SOCO and adhere to it.
- Use messaging to provide the media factual "grabs" or "tweets," outlining what, who, when, where, why and how in sound bites of 30 words maximum.
- Prepare questions and answers, fast facts, media releases and blogs.
- Post media releases to the website within one hour of the occurrence of a newsworthy event.

Coming out of Crisis

"It's like wrestling a gorilla. You rest when the gorilla rests."
–Michael Regester & Judy Larkin

Returning to Board Direction and Line Management

Following the resolution of a crisis situation, organizations may quickly return to line management or commence interim operations in a disaster recovery center.

Regaining its former commercial position, however, may take the organization some time. Organizations may return to normal line management but will not regain their commercial position immediately, as shareholder value in the wake of corporate crises historically takes up to 50 days to recover.

The initial loss of shareholder value in the wake of corporate crises historically averages 5% for those that recover and 11% for those that do not recover.

While those organizations that recover see a 5% increase by the 50th trading day, non-recovering organizations experience losses as high as 15% up to one year later.

Typically, Board members, crisis leaders, and emergency managers may employ a variety of euphemisms to describe the progress of the organization's recovery.

These expressions are indicative of specific styles of thinking that are characteristic of the approach particular to that individual or position:

- The Board may use such expressions as "it will be this way" when seeking to transform from crisis situations.

- Crisis leaders use expressions such as "I see it happening this way" when morphing out of crisis, which is often indicative of "back to the future" thinking.

- Emergency managers may use such expressions as "the plan is working" when emergency situations are returning to normal, which is indicative of "back to the past" thinking.

"The most pathetic person in the world is someone who has sight but no vision."

–Helen Keller

CHAPTER 3

Information Pull and Information Push

Information Capture and Transfer (ICATS)

> *Difficulties come in waves; no one can resist the avalanche of problems to be solved or information to be distributed.*

Log-keeping is a critical function for all teams, and as such, must be entrusted to a senior member of the organization. A log-keeper or historian maintains an accurate, written record and should not be confused with the scribe or board writer, who displays visual information to aid pictorial thinking. In a team hamstrung by staff shortages, the log-keeper should be retained at the expense of the scribe.

In some circumstances, team discussion may be excluded from the log and any associated documents may be marked "Legal Professional Privilege". This generally occurs if those documents or the team's discussion involves the provision or receipt of legal advice and will occur at the discretion of the team leader.

In anticipation of a post-crisis inquiry and the possibility of team members providing evidence to an investigator or regulator, cautionary steps may be required. Team members could be called on to recount the efforts of the organization in crisis avoidance or management and offer comment on whether the organization appeared capable of responding effectively.

Some crisis situations will necessitate the crisis team's collection of all working documentation every few hours. The crisis leader may even employ the organization's lawyers to vet all external communications, or indeed to act as log-keepers.

While log-keepers may vary in their methods and the tools they employ, accurate and comprehensive recording is the essence. Whatever the tools of preference—pencil and paper, laptop and printer, or Virtual Crisis Leadership Environments in the cloud, such as the incident management system from MissionMode—it is crucial that a transcript be available at all times and that updates can be affected with ease and rapidity.

Technology can present attractive options for electronic log-keeping in operations rooms. It can provide the ability to keep an accurate log that can be distributed securely and in real-time to those who need it. However, ensure that you rehearse using the technology, and that the information provided is appropriate to those who need it.

Ineffective management procedures for critical information requirements include a failure:

- to post or display them in a conspicuous and timely manner
- to update them once answered
- of decision makers to recognize when information requirements have been answered

The log is a written chronological record of all activities. It contains the company's record of events, decisions, and process; and it may become a legal document subject to internal investigations and external inquiries.

Thus, log-keepers must have a clear understanding of their duties and responsibilities and be frequently rehearsed in their ability to record the team's interaction with multiple stakeholders simultaneously.

As time allows, the log-keeper may record a timed schedule of reporting deadlines from details supplied by the team and monitor compliance with those deadlines. If further time allows, the log-keeper also may record a schedule of agreed commitments and then monitor the schedule to ensure the team is reminded of those commitments.

Communicating across teams is a key challenge.

In meeting the challenges presented by information overload, log-keepers must understand the team decision making and problem-solving process and how to optimize information tools in recording and prioritizing information.

They must use a practiced format to handle, prioritize, and record information from multiple stakeholders simultaneously. This will enable them to multitask—listen to multiple conversations, screen, prioritize, and record the critical information.

Communicating horizontally and across teams is a key challenge to rapid crisis response. Focus on who needs to know what and whether technology can bridge the gap between people being in different locations.

A common operating picture can only really be provided quickly using technology. A common fault is that the log-keeper creates the log in isolation and it is not available to others during a crisis.

	Same Time	Different Times
Same Place	What has happened	Deadlines
Different Places	What is happening now	Commitments

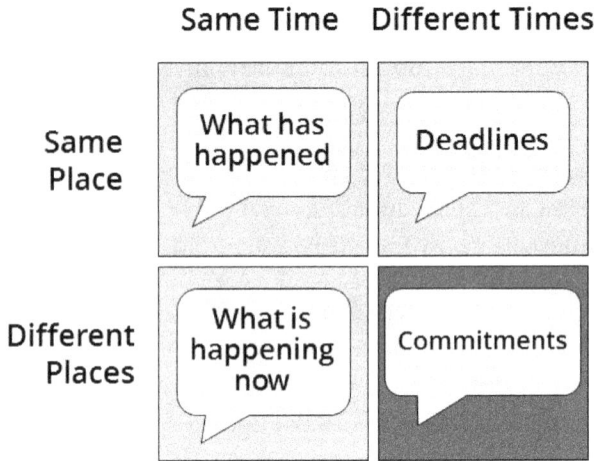

Optimize information tools to record and prioritize information

Fighting for and Controlling Crisis Information

A well thought-out plan, even when supported by capable command and control technology and systems, must be executed by personnel who are trained and understand how to use information to accomplish the task.

Effective communication systems are absolutely vital, but they may be among the first casualties of a crisis. Jammed communications are a distinctive feature of a crisis and may be an important initial indicator of an emergent crisis situation.

Have a backup plan for your normal methods of communication. If you normally use the corporate Internet connection, get an alternative connection, such as ADSL or 3G, that is separate and ideally mobile.

It is crucial that the organization possess the ability to return to basic means of communication and is not solely dependent on state-of-the-art technology. A telephone filtering and message-taking capability is critical; the crisis team must understand the flow of information into, around and out of its designated facility.

Of primary importance is the team members' understanding of how to rectify any disruption to this information flow. One particularly effective means to overcome the problem of jammed communications is the team's ability to pool mobile phones.

Team email or crisis management software should be the primary conduit for internal communication, so that telephones are freed for external communication.

The line numbers for any telephones in the team room should not be divulged without the team leader's approval, as these telephones may be used as an open line by a critical stakeholder.

Telephones in the team room should be direct lines with silent, unlisted numbers, as this presents the best guarantee of secure communication. The use of mobile phones should not be permitted during team sessions, as individual calls may detract from the collective nature of the team's primary purpose.

The advantage of crisis management software is that team communications are secure, fast, concurrent, distributed and controlled. It is able to provide a common operating picture to all invited stakeholders.

The call center is the most efficient channel for filtering and taking messages, and it should be permitted to perform its designated function. If, on the other hand, team members choose to call stakeholders, this will be as a result of a team decision or at the instigation of the team leader. Personal calls only should be made from the team facility in an emergency or during a team breakout.

Business support teams should act as an information conduit for the crisis team. This will allow the core business of managing the crisis to continue uninterrupted.

Operating the Call Center

The organization's internal telephone filtering and message-taking capability normally is based on the existing switchboard or reception-ist. Regardless of the level of technology that has been invested in a switchboard, it may be unable to cope with the conduct of normal business operations in addition to crisis communication.

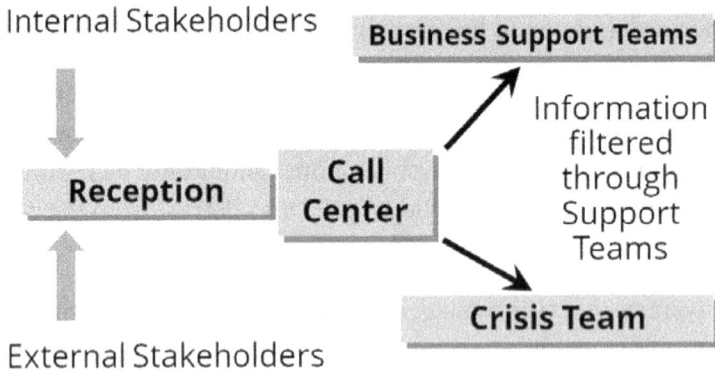

The system of telephone response

The organization may be forced to minimize the operation of unaf-fected components of the business in order to prevent logjams.

Crisis calls that are attended by the switchboard should be directed to the deputy team leader—or the appropriate communications support team, HR support team, or subordinate Emergency Management team, if activated.

Initial telephone procedure should be described in some detail in the crisis plan. The deputy leader must be responsive to the dynamic crisis environment and implement change as the need arises. They must act quickly to establish the required protocol to suit the rapidly emerging situation; block and log often.

Given the vital nature of the organization's call management, telephone responders are often pooled from senior managers to record messages on carbonized message pads.

Calls that cannot be managed by telephone responders, either because of the nature of information sought or the identity of the caller, are referred immediately to the deputy team leader. Telephone responders should refer such messages in hard copy, using the top copy of the carbonized log.

The deputy leader will then pass this message to the most appropriate member of the crisis team, either in team session or during a time-out. The second copy is retained for inclusion in support team records. Once the return call has been made, an annotation to this effect should be made on the top copy of the log before it is returned to the appropriate telephone responder.

Telephone responders must be updated regularly on developments and "releasable information," both within the emerging crisis and in the crisis team's strategy, as they are effectively the first line of defense. The deputy leader performs this vital function, which is best achieved through a single conduit.

The Role of Telephone Responders

The role of telephone responders is to manage calls with courtesy and efficiency, directing the caller immediately to the appropriate authority.

Crises necessarily incur an enormous volume of calls, particularly in the initial stages. The crisis situation will impose considerable pressure on all staff, many of whom will be relocated from their normal work-space.

Members of support teams will be especially vulnerable to the stress of dis–location, as they may occupy designated areas away from their usual office environment.

The call center should be activated as soon as practicable in order to cope with the initial response to the crisis, both internal and external. An extraordinary range of callers can be expected during a crisis, and it is vital that the call center be briefed on the appropriate authority to respond and the precise identity of the respondent.

Telephone responders should not answer queries relating to the crisis or provide information, unless specifically directed to and supplied with clear instructions on the release of information.

This is particularly important when the source of a query is a relative or next of kin of any injured or deceased persons. Telephone respond-ers should insist on the timely provision of such information if it is not forthcoming through normal channels.

Calls made directly to individual offices, rather than through the switchboard, may be left unanswered or diverted automatically to another number. An automated answering system with an interactive voice recording may also be a useful option in a crisis situation. Ideally, unmanned phones should be diverted to a telephone responder or directly to the call center.

Essential procedures for managing the call center include:

- Activating telephone responders and the use of carbonized log sheets.

- Fighting for information. Staff should
    - telephone key points within the workplace to determine whether colleagues are at normal workstations where calls can be taken,
    - confirm which support teams are operating and what calls they will take, and
    - be briefed on where calls are to be directed for media, relatives, VIP, financial and normal business queries.

- Providing a web address or taking messages when managers cannot be contacted, rather than providing call-back numbers.

- Staff must ensure that promised call-backs are made.

- Managing all calls with courtesy and efficiency. Staff must remain calm, even when callers are rude.

- Supervisors must be informed of any unusual or very difficult calls and staff must take a break when feeling stressed or under constant pressure.

- Providing alternatives to callers. Should members of the call center find themselves overwhelmed by the sheer volume of calls, a ready response should indicate an alternative to the caller.

- Ideally, call center staff should take the caller's name and number and return the call as soon as practical.

- Ensuring that staff avoids divulging any information on the crisis unless specifically directed by the supervisor as part of the organization's crisis strategy.

- Reminding staff never to provide crisis team room telephone numbers to callers.

Virtual Crisis Leadership Environments

Connect, Communicate, Continue

The term "virtual crisis leadership environment" (VCLE) is used to describe virtual preparedness for crises. Information-centered organizations create a great number of channels in order to move information faster.

VCLE seeks to optimize communication and information systems through:

- Virtual Private Networks (VPNs) and web logs (blogs)
- Crisis portals to inform travelling team members
- Crisis management software for collaboration amongst geographically-separated business teams
- Emergency notification software
- Access to social media to understand what the Internet world is saying
- Toll-free numbers for public hotlines on particular issues
- Switchboards that allow for a cascading system of answering multiple calls
- Business support team email addresses for 24-hour communications
- "Dark" websites, which can be activated to replace normal sites for media releases and fast facts

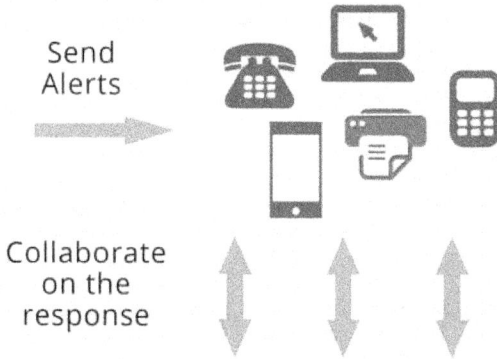

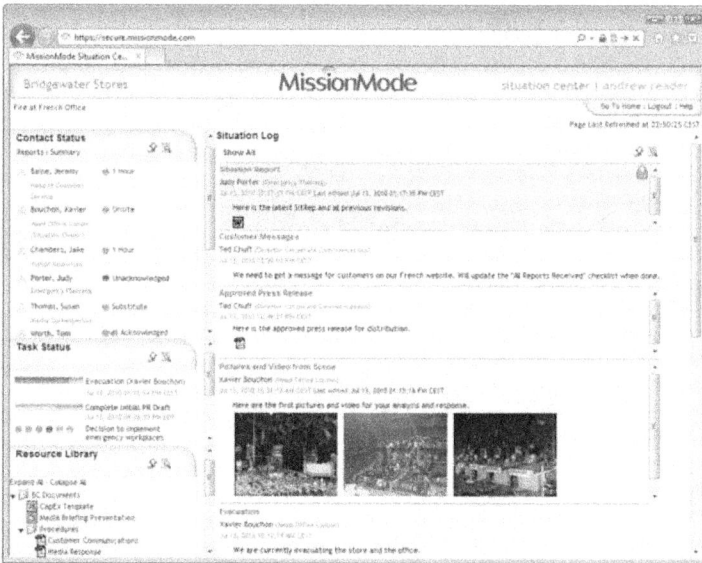

One type of VCLE is an incident/crisis management system that enables coordination and communication amongst teams in any location.

VCLE can sometimes be manpower intensive, so the organization must always be prepared to go back to basics in crisis situations. Organizations with prepared business continuity plans may integrate a disaster recovery center into their VCLE for a fast transition to interim operations.

Sites are described in terms of the level of organizational information stored:

- Cold sites require user organizations to bring their information with them

- Warm sites already store some of the organization's information

- Hot sites contain constantly replicated information; they may also operate in a dispersed mode, with data in a variety of locations

Every crisis has an Internet component.

CHAPTER 4

Courage and Determination

Crisis leadership and commercial bravery:
surfing on the front of the wave

The Role of the Board and Future Directions

> *"Character is not made in a crisis, it is only exhibited."*
> *–Robert Freeman*

Restoring stakeholder trust and confidence in an organization, and providing direction on continuous disclosure to the market and Stock Exchange requires exceptional leadership qualities.

The requirement for such qualities is starkly apparent given that corporate strategies focus on exploiting opportunities in the ever-shifting environment in which business operates.

Crisis leadership simply equates to the formulation and implementation of strategies for managing threats and handling disruptive organizational change. It is thus increasingly becoming incorporated into the organization's modus operandi as a strategic planning tool.

Directors generally accept crisis leadership as a corporate governance strategy to safeguard financial, environmental and social bottom lines. The public expects higher standards of corporate behavior overall, and the impact of globalization is forcing organizations to formulate international policies, so the Board actively prepares strategies to combat crises. It is all about high accountability and low control.

In any given crisis there is a constant handoff between the crisis leader, normally the Chief Executive, and the Board of Directors. As the opening quote from the book noted, failure is not an option for these crisis directors.

Whereas crisis leaders have only choices, crisis directors must use their spheres of influence to direct the organization out of the crisis or away from an impending crisis. These crisis directors are an anonymous team of business leaders, independent from the crisis team process of developing and implementing crisis strategy.

While crisis teams focus on verification and application, Boards provide vision and decision.

Joint Venture Crisis Leadership

Joint ventures require arrangements for joint venture crisis teams to meet at neutral venues so that individual member organizations can protect their own interests. The joint venture crisis team may find itself hamstrung in its strategies unless it is vested with the executive authority of all members of the joint venture.

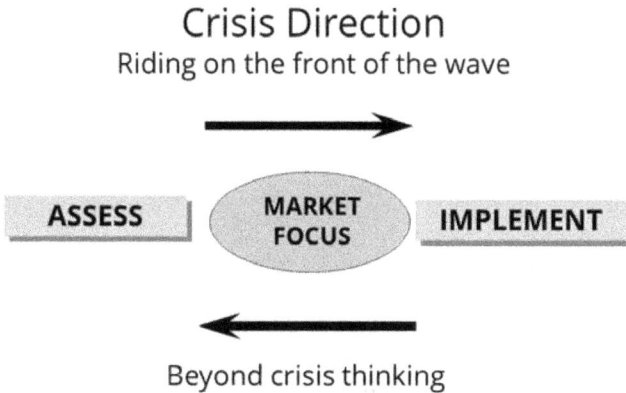

Crisis Direction
Riding on the front of the wave

ASSESS MARKET FOCUS IMPLEMENT

Beyond crisis thinking

The crisis team may also find itself precluded from making public statements concerning a crisis situation in any of the entities that are controlled by, or linked to, the joint venture without direct approval of the member organizations.

Commercial Bravery

Crisis leadership is about seizing the initiative and taking control of a situation before it engulfs the organization. Organizations have few friends in a crisis, but they must exhibit raw leadership.

The fundamental job of the leader is to enforce strategy and to resist leadership compression by thinking "Horizons not borders, solutions not differences, and challenges not barriers."

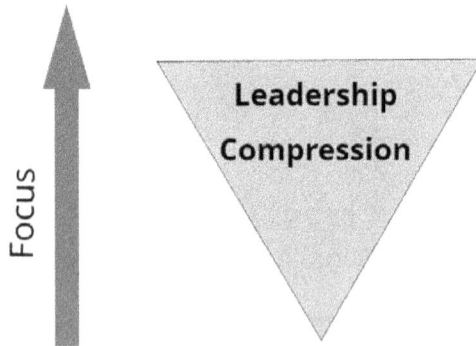

Resisting event fixation and the tactical urge

Crisis leaders require decisiveness and commercial bravery when friendly stakeholders may be neutral at best, and there may be a variety of competitors seeking to take advantage of a crisis situation.

"Leaders are dealers in hope." – Napoleon

During a crisis, the leader's competencies sharpen in definition. The leader must retain control of their emotions at all times, using them as appropriate to the situation.

The human face of the leader is one of their most valuable tools and must be used sparingly and effectively—particularly for vital personnel issues.

Personal face time cannot be deputized, and leaders must be aware of the negative ramifications of appearing impersonal and uncaring. Leaders also must maintain their ability to think clearly in a crisis and not become entangled in the swirl of anxiety that crises engender.

Above all, leaders are responsible for developing strategy and articulating it to their organization. Strong leadership is fundamental to any successful strategy, as it is about choices and trade-offs, and involves every aspect of business operation.

Heroes do not, however, make good crisis leaders, and team leaders should not be afraid to ask advice and receive a contrary opinion. "Captainitis" is failure by crisis leaders to seek or consider contrary advice.

When low-level issues or workplace emergencies escalate to crisis proportions, it is often as a result of the actions of line managers who try to resolve these issues themselves or refuse to recognize the burgeoning crisis.

In the past, it has been traditional for managers to consider that requesting assistance to resolve an issue would be perceived as failure on their part.

Under current management practices, however, it is considered the norm for managers to employ prudent over-reaction as a caution against a lurking crisis and to seek opportunities to transform rather than simply survive.

Raw Leadership

As anxiety is contagious, so is serenity. Panic is contagious, and leadership, too.

Business crises are an environment where trial-and-error, ambiguity, and evolving ends are the norm. These situations demand an adaptive mental stance, adaptive approaches to problem solving, and bold action to create opportunity in ambiguous circumstances.

This comes though study of crises and practice in real or simulated circumstances, reinforced by natural talent.

Leaders must maintain their ability to think clearly during an emergent crisis rather than becoming swept up in the panic of crisis hysteria. Theirs is the crucial task of developing a strategy aimed at resolution and articulating it to their organization through raw displays of leadership in the workplace.

In the first 30 seconds of meeting someone, a person will typically make 42 opinions or judgments of the person met. This has much to do with survival, the premier instinct in humans. It is therefore paramount in leadership projection in crises.

The perceptions made of a leader by their team, even when they walk back in the room after a time out, may be critical to further performance. Look out—they are watching you!

Crisis leadership will manage and take advantage of the future— especially when it comes at you faster than you can manage it, and sometimes all at once.

Among the best practices to reduce stress and overcome the common crisis feelings of flight, fight or freeze is the use of a colleague to observe and offer encouragement. Leaders need good self-maintenance skills to balance crisis deadlines with the personal ability to cope.

Negative or anxious thoughts can be controlled through mental discipline and the use of enforced breaks from the pressured environment. These need not be lengthy in duration and may simply mean five minutes away from the crisis team and the situation or operations rooms.

Leaders often need to remind themselves of their own strengths and the crises they have managed in the past. Focusing on the future also helps leaders to regain their perspective in an environment that may be weighted in the unfolding of a drama in rapidly changing intervals.

Physical relaxation measures such as office exercises and stretching can also help to refocus a leader's mind under pressure. Leaders who talk to themselves often find that this quickly becomes self-critical and may reinforce the fear of failure. Discussing strategies and crucial issues with key colleagues may assist in defusing any feelings of inadequacy.

Executive Combat

> "I kept six honest serving-men. They taught me all I knew. Their names were What and Why and When and How and Where and Who." – Rudyard Kipling

Crisis leadership requires teamwork to manage the unexpected and unforeseen within a crisis environment. To guard against brain lock and group think, the team should be small enough so as to be effective, large enough to be representative, and have the seniority to be compelling. The team must be able to think big, think fast and think ahead.

Team members with different perspectives must be vocal members of the group, as crisis leadership requires all individuals to combine effectively as a team. Team members would do well to remember that they are effectively earning their salaries in one day.

With crisis leadership, truth is the primary value. Opinion is also a team asset and, while the team will comprise a mix of introverts and extroverts, no opinion should be silenced or punished. All team members should have the freedom to comment in order to raise the level of team dialogue. The exertion of pressure on team members to conform to a general consensus view could lead to the failure to consider all options.

Team leaders should be wary of the business adviser who appears to intimately understand the intricacies of the crisis. Under pressure in a team environment, this individual may aspire to take over as crisis leader.

> *"Everyone has a plan until he gets punched in the face."*
> *– Popularly attributed to Mike Tyson*

The team must also take care in selecting its legal counsel and should opt for a lawyer who does not work in secrecy, can work quickly, and can assimilate into a team with a Corporate Affairs component.

Less successful crisis leadership has often been characterized by disagreement between lawyers and the organization's Corporate Affairs representatives, with critical, and often very public, results.

Corporate Affairs members will naturally advocate telling it all, telling it fast, and telling it truthfully. Lawyers, on the other hand, will often advocate saying nothing, doing nothing and admitting nothing.

Crisis leaders must ensure that lawyers do not slow the crisis agenda. Leaders must be prepared to take sound legal advice but must avoid being gagged on disclosure, as many lawyers, like accountants, tend to seek the known position. The legal fraternity is trained to seek safety, and trained to give that advice, which considers even the remotest risk of an unforeseen disaster.

> *"The first thing we do, let's kill all the lawyers."*
> *–Shakespeare in Henry VI*

A common perception is that lawyers tend to find problems rather than resolve them, while the Corporate Affairs member may frequently manage variations of the organization's key themes.

In the world of Corporate Affairs, perceptions and illusions are equally, if not more, important than facts and reality. Team leaders must be conscious of the pressure under which Corporate Affairs operates, but likewise cognizant that crisis leadership is more than external relations.

The Strategic Management of Emergencies

While an emergency constitutes any abnormal or non-routine event, 95% of emergencies will never escalate to crisis level. Crises that effectively bypass the escalation process and erupt without warning are of greatest concern to the organization.

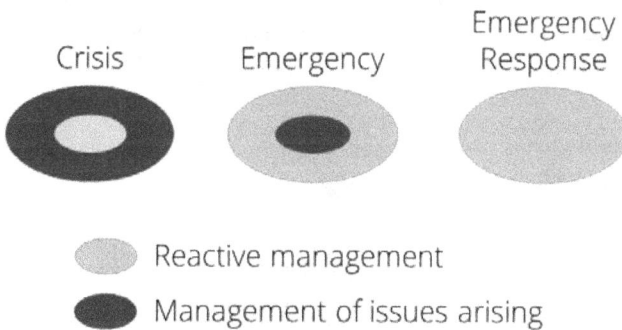

Crisis   Emergency   Emergency
                                    Response

Reactive management
Management of issues arising

Crisis and Emergency Management system

Emergency managers necessarily focus on extraordinary tasks such as saving lives, containing property damage, minimizing data loss, and protecting the environment. This requires multi-disciplined skills, such as those inherent in professional response agencies, to manage disasters at local, state and national levels.

The handing-off of crisis issues that prove to be beyond the resources of an emergency manager is a critical procedure. To ensure that a two-way flow of information occurs, crisis leaders and emergency managers often exchange staff so they can remain abreast of events in all areas.

While the management of a major emergency may only dominate the organization's operations for several hours or days, crises can last much longer before the organization survives, transforms or fails.

Emergency management concerns the resolution of yesterday's problem, while crisis leadership is anchored in the resolution of an evolving problem through second-stage thought.

Smaller organizations, however, may have to combine their strategic and tactical focus into a one-team approach to manage emergencies that develop into crises. Effecting this combination can require a delicate touch, as any confusion of the two approaches may diminish the organization's strategic focus at the corporate level.

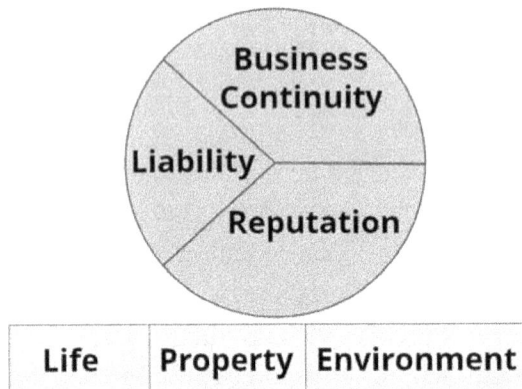

Identifying crisis issues and emergency tasks

This situation may also create unreal expectations of tactical managers who are best utilized at the lower level in security, emergency response or safety matters.

In the transition from line management, emergency managers:

- Should activate the emergency management team, call center and business support teams, then adjust the business support team response if the crisis team is also activated.
- Must insist on constant information updates and the provision of vital facts surrounding the protection of life, property, data, and the environment.
- Must utilize updates to brainstorm and prioritize key tasks.
- Transfer responsibility for business continuity, reputation, and liability issues to the crisis team, and implement a work plan to regain control of the event.
- Must respond to approaches from the media by providing reassurances, asserting control, displaying commitment, and demonstrating that affected people and the environment are the organization's first priority.

Critical Thinking in Emergencies

> *"The darkest corner in hell is reserved for fence-sitters."*
> *–Dante*

Emergency management is like a sine wave. If there is too much action, there is a danger of acting too rashly. If there is too much planning, there is a danger of over-analyzing and, thus failing to act. It is all about the balance between acting and analyzing.

It is a unique emergency manager who can rapidly assimilate enough diverse information to make anticipatory decisions. Machines alone will not produce increased leadership ability without an accompanying increase in the emergency manager's ability to make decisions and issue orders.

The sine wave of Emergency Management

The characteristics of emergency management teams are as follows:

- A group with a multi-disciplined approach that can mobilize quickly for organization when facing failure
- An ability to gather and share information quickly and then arrive at an immediate course of action or to hand-off the information to senior management
- An ability to manipulate and monitor resources to implement decisions

> *"However carefully an organization goes through the steps and however well drawn its emergency plans are, it is the Emergency Management team's proficiency that will achieve success and efficiency and ultimately determine the organization's reputation when a threat materializes and becomes a major event."*
>
> *– John Laye*

Leading People under Stress

Crises call for someone with answers, decisions, strength, and a map of the future, someone who knows where we ought to be going. In short, someone who can make hard problems seem simple.

Fundamentally, success in business, like in war, is based on leadership. Other factors—such as information, preparation, organization, communication, motivation, and execution—also contribute to success. The effectiveness of these factors, however, is entirely determined by the quality of leadership provided.

The crisis leader or the HR member should inform all staff of the strategies the organization is employing to manage the crisis and seek to use the organization's employees to competitive advantage. Staff must be aware of the identity of the designated traditional and social spokesperson and strategies for fielding and forwarding inquiries. They need to believe that the organization is in control of the crisis.

In a crisis situation, the role of the leader is often to implement strategies that offer people a way through the crisis by either rejecting the past entirely or integrating the past, with change through bold new ideas.

Crisis situations will create an atmosphere of confusion and lead to stress and anxiety, which will affect employees in varying ways, as not everyone will be able to personally manage the effects of stress.

Some employees do not develop the symptoms of stress until the crisis is over. They may become self-critical and direct criticism towards those colleagues whom they perceived to have performed poorly. Many employees will be unable to accept that they may have been affected by a form of crisis-induced stress.

Leaders must develop counseling strategies and implement post-traumatic care regimens to rectify any residual effects of the crisis within the organization's staff. Employees should also be permitted to seek professional stress counseling on a confidential basis and with the full support of management and peers.

CHAPTER 5

Controlling and Delivering Perceptions

The Single Overriding Communications Objective

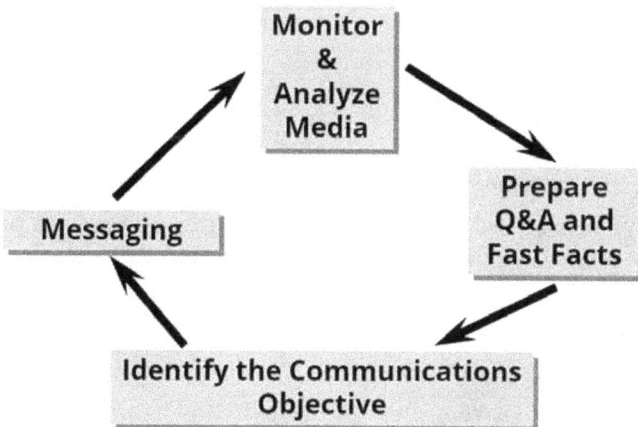

Media Management – Monitor, Analyze & Respond

> *Reputation is something you do when someone is watching. Character is what you do when no one is watching.*

In the information age, with 53% of value in companies in intangible assets, you need a large stock of media good will to survive and prosper. Understand that journalists apply a narrow focus of approach to your wide business. In the media world, two data points makes a trend. To guide that trend, get the media as a partner and not an adversary.

Crises are complex events requiring a stretched capacity. To look past the zone of horror, seize the first-moving advantage through fast and full analysis, and then communicate to fill the vacuum. Use a truth squad to monitor the media, corroborate, and check. Use employees as brand ambassadors.

Be aware that perception is often at odds with the truth. It is important to gauge it objectively and manage it effectively. Trust and truth are the currency of the 21st Century and there is a difference between responsibility and liability.

There is no legal risk in apologizing, and with media as a partner it will present major opportunities. Good news stays local, but a crisis anywhere is a crisis everywhere. You can expect to be a story every day, everywhere; so add social media to your crisis team, as print and TV reporters will use social media to keep up.

It is the role of the communications support team to control and deliver crisis perceptions, seeking to mitigate and overcome the traditional media's 'shock-gasp-horror' news formulae. In order to achieve this, the team must:

- Ensure that members are fully briefed on all the facts. Team members will check the accuracy and reliability of all available factual information.

- Assess what additional media support is required. The team will establish the communications support team room as a virtual press office and commence log-keeping.

- Arrange media monitoring and recording of news. The team will analyze media coverage through its source, content, medium, and effect (SCAME) as well as its strength, weakness, opportunity or threat (SWOT).

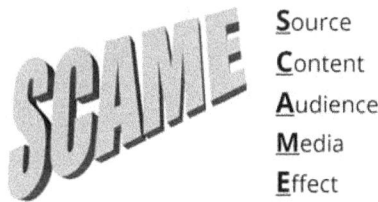

Source
Content
Audience
Media
Effect

- Determine the media response strategy in consultation with the Corporate Affairs member and maintain contact with the crisis team.

- Brief the call center on how to respond to incoming stakeholder calls and preparation to field such calls.

- Brief building security and reception on the management of visitors.

- Liaise with the crisis leader on whether statements have been released. The team will then obtain copies and coordinate the release of further statements.

- Continually brief the call center and other business support teams on releasable information.

- Arrange traditional media conferences, engage social media and support executives moving to the site of the crisis. The team will write the initial statement, Q&A, rehearse the spokesperson, and distribute fast facts, photos, and footage to the media.
- Implement the longer-term media campaign.
- Monitor stress within the communications support team itself.

First Contact with Electronic and Non-Electronic Media

"Four hostile newspapers are more feared than a thousand bayonets."

–Napoleon Bonaparte

The communications support team should be careful to greet and contain media representatives when they arrive. Buy time, if necessary, by leaving them in the care of team members while statements are prepared elsewhere or by postponing any scheduled statement.

Media representatives must not be left alone, as they will seize the opportunity to interview employees, contractors, eyewitnesses, Emergency Services or industry commentators, and any other interested bystanders. Should members of the media seek information by telephone, the telephone responder should establish their query and deadline and buy time by advising that the organization's spokesperson will reply.

The communications support team should then develop the SOCO and call the media outlet. The team should monitor the results and be ready to respond to any inaccuracies.

The communications support team must take the initiative in breaking the news of the crisis to selected media. The team must be proactive and consistent in its dealings with media. The communications support team is also responsible for monitoring subsequent traditional and social media coverage and communicating quickly and directly with key stakeholders.

The order of notification priority should be:

1. those who should respond, such as Emergency Services and the crisis team
2. those who must comment, such as spokespersons and government officials
3. those with a special need-to-know, such as stock analysts, customers, suppliers, employees, victims, and their families and unions
4. the broadcast and print media
5. the general public.

This is an effective strategy to manage the media response by tailoring the scope of the information divulged and it also acts to protect the organization by buying time to properly develop crisis strategy.

Messaging, Blogging and Tweeting

"In the court of public opinion, a person or organization is guilty until proven innocent." –K. Fearn-Banks

It is vital that the organization's key messages be communicated in short, sharp media-friendly statements. Messaging is formulating the SOCO in three or four key sentences, which can be delivered clearly and with impact. The aim of messaging is to fill the vacuum, enabling the organization to regain the initiative.

During crisis situations it is imperative to produce the organization's factual message, dispelling rumors and speculation. The media must be given the full picture, as quickly as possible.

Given the emotion of a breaking story and an emerging crisis, great care must be taken in the development of the message. Issues crucial to the organization, particularly those impacted by the crisis, must be managed in a relevant and sympathetic manner.

Such issues must also be accorded the appropriate priority, especially in a public forum. Key priorities for any organization must remain people, environment, property, and money in that order.

All Q&A opportunities should be used by the traditional spokesperson to reinforce the communications objective. The communications objective will not provide an answer to every question, but it can be incorporated into almost every answer by a skillful spokesperson. Q&A is an excellent formula for providing basic information.

The team spokesperson must remain calm under intense media pressure. This is always a significant challenge for even the most practiced operators. The use of key messages is an essential strategy for a spokesperson. These messages must be simple, memorable, and answer the media's critical questions, as follows:

- What happened?
- Who is involved?
- When did it happen?
- Where did it occur?
- Why did happen?
- How will it be prevented from happening again?

The communications support team should be cautious in its use of media conferences as a means of implementing the organization's reputation strategy. Media conferences present an opportunity to deliver a message to a large body of media representatives and ensure that the organization retains control of the agenda.

The communications support team should not, however, schedule a media conference until a robust strategy has been developed. Media conferences should always be scheduled on the hour, as many media outlets will employ live crosses during the hourly news updates.

Beware that with the increasing prevalence of social media, Internet news and 24 hour news channels, the time to act is being compressed. To win control of the agenda from the media is crucial. Using technology to provide a robust and quick internal communications channel to react, decide and communicate information is a key to staying ahead of the media and other stakeholders.

> *"Does anyone have any questions for the answers I am about to give?" – Henry Kissinger*

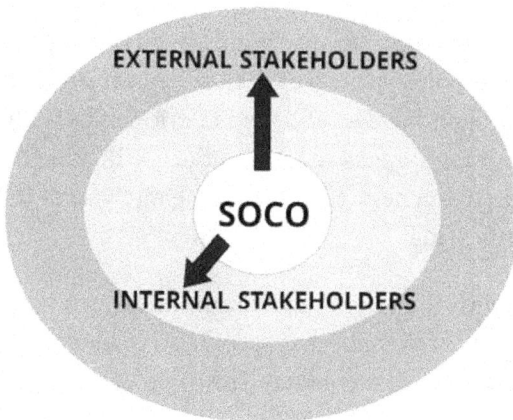

Media Monitoring and Analysis

Monitor, analyze, and respond

Continuous monitoring is essential in the successful management of a crisis. Facts triumph over opinion. The main task of the communications support team is to determine the communications objective through analysis of the media. Analysis must be completed quickly as the message heard by the stakeholder must be that of an organization's spokesperson rather than the observations of the mass media.

One particularly useful strategy is the employment of "ground truthing" or listening posts. Ground truthing refers to the active gathering of intelligence at the grassroots level, similar to buzz or viral marketing feedback.

In a media context, this may be achieved by using members of the communications support team to seek the opinion of journalists and other stakeholders off the record. Media monitoring equates to the truth squad.

This strategy is useful for monitoring rumors and speculation, although it is often only effective when members of the communications support team have established relationships with media representatives. Making face to face contact with stakeholders to ground truth media generates speed in the analysis of information, and in communicating.

In any dealing with the media, the communications support team must be cognizant of the fact that speed and evidence of reputation building behavior is of the essence. The opposite is spin, equating to "No action and talk only" (NATO).

This need for speed is particularly the case if the level of organizational exposure to the media is high as a result of the crisis situation.

The communications support team may employ Public Relations consultants who offer media monitoring services, but the support team must be confident that these consultants can maintain the organization's crisis tempo.

The point at which the organization ceases to be the main focus of media attention is a dangerous juncture, as the media may begin to seek out new angles for stories. These new angles may be predominantly based on hearsay, rumor, and speculation, leading to misinformation and confusion.

The communications support team must be able to predict the point at which media attention will begin to waver and members of the team must prepare fresh information in order to focus the media on the key messages underpinning the strategies that the organization wishes to articulate.

Releasing Media Statements

> Communications is not what you send out, but what arrives, and the gap exposes a company to media decisions.

The initial media statement should be outlined as a template in the organization's crisis plan. The media statement may be written by the crisis leader, or they may task the Corporate Affairs member to do so. The media statement must be based on information derived from the organization's fact sheets and must not contain speculation.

The statement should, however, indicate the organization's concern for its employees and shareholders and reassure these and other stakeholders that it retains control. The statement should be communicated using simple, concise language.

The crisis leader should note the existence of any agreements with partners in contractual arrangements that may govern the delivery of event-related messages. The crisis leader should also remain cognizant of the requirement for prior clearance with regulatory authorities. Speak within your pay grade.

At the same time, they must be conscious that delays in the internal approval of media releases may result in major problems in image control and information flow. The first media statement should be drafted and be able to be released no more than one hour after the declaration of a crisis situation.

Indeed, the ability to immediately post media releases to a website has re-defined the standard for crisis response. Communications support teams must have the ability to immediately remove the existing website and replace it with a single click message at any time of the day or night. Connect, communicate and continue.

The Spokesperson – Angles, Attitude, and Audience.

Rational messages persuade. Emotional messages motivate.

The crisis plan must nominate an organizational spokesperson. This is a role normally filled by the crisis leader or the Corporate Affairs member. This individual must be prepared to face the media around the clock, as most media outlets will seek a statement at a time not of the organization's choosing.

The communications support team and the spokesperson must aim to win control of the agenda from the media and must also maintain the belief that the war of words can ultimately be won.

Every item of factual substance that can be included in the initial media statement will ease the pressure on the spokesperson and the communications support team. Silence is not an option that can be considered in the face of confusing advice and contradictory evidence.

The organization must prepare its most credible and knowledgeable spokesperson to address stakeholders on demand. This is the only effective strategy to:

- prevent speculation
- answer critics
- ensure accuracy
- prevent incurring media hostility

The media may seek an interview by phone or may ambush the spokesperson as they leave their office. The spokesperson must be able to manage information by themselves, albeit with prescriptive direction on more sensitive aspects of the chosen strategy.

These aspects are best covered in written and rehearsed Q&A which includes such topics as industrial relations, previous prosecutions of organization members, and the organization's accident history.

The team spokesperson should have a sound knowledge of and an easy familiarity with the prepared Q&A, the organization's profile and statistics, and pre-packaged "media to go." The spokesperson should determine the duration and theme of the interview or media conference beforehand and rigidly adhere to those arrangements.

There is no more tangible way to demonstrate an organization's level of effective control than scrutiny of its performance under a barrage of media inquiries.

A well-prepared spokesperson should have nothing to fear from media questions. The questions themselves will not embarrass the organization's senior executives and stakeholders, but an unsatisfactory answer may.

The human brain works off impressions, not facts. Hence 55% of what a target audience thinks comes from your look, and 38% from your sounds. Maintain eye contact and turn the camera on in people's minds. It is all about preparation, attitude, control and expression.

Adopt a dressing room mentality to overcome nervousness. Use SOCO to bridge from questions to answers in order to "block and score runs."

Question = Answer + SOCO (the position you want)

Should a spokesperson be ambushed by media representatives before they feel adequately prepared to comment, they should keep moving, isolate on the topic, and schedule a media engagement at the earliest possible date and time, subject to the organization's preferred topical boundaries.

Coming out of Crisis – Back to Public Relations

You cannot manage what you cannot measure.

The communications support team may employ the following campaign tools when morphing out of crises over the longer-term. The focus is on outcomes, not outputs:

- Lines of persuasion: key messages which may prompt the stakeholder to respond in the manner required. Any key message must be expressed in three points or fewer.
- Themes and symbols: news grabs and quotes which feature the advantages and benefits of the message.

- Intensity and timing of media exposure: this often depends on the stakeholder's access and susceptibility to different types of media and should strike a balance between repetition and saturation.
- Key performance indicators: these indicators reveal whether the stakeholder is responding, for example, through a decrease in the number of complaints or the receipt of favorable reports.

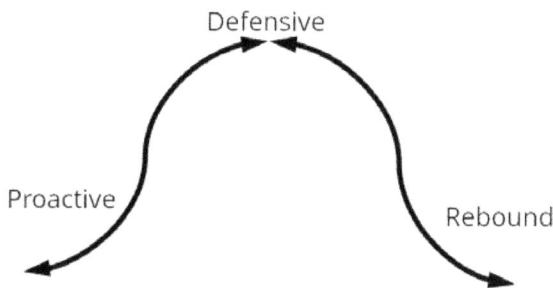

Defensive

Proactive

Rebound

Lifecycle of an issue

Outcomes, not Outputs

Each morning PR professionals wake up. They know they must talk fast or be left behind. Each morning journalists wake up. They know they must get the story first or be left behind, as some 60,000 messages hit the human brain between waking up and going to sleep.

> *A crisis is more than just appearing in the news for three days in a row. Crisis Management 101 is core business.*

CHAPTER 6

Communicating with Affected People

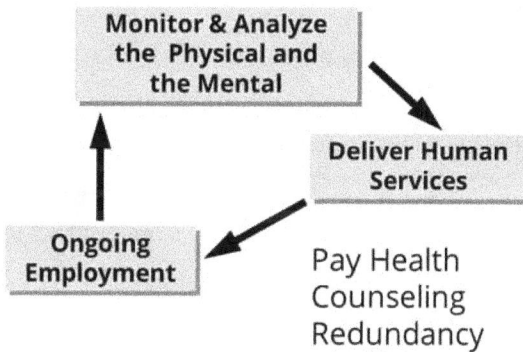

```
        ┌─────────────────┐
        │ Monitor & Analyze│
        │ the Physical and │ ──┐
        │   the Mental     │   │
        └─────────────────┘   ▼
              ▲          ┌──────────────┐
              │          │ Deliver Human│
              │          │   Services   │
        ┌──────────┐     └──────────────┘
        │ Ongoing  │ ◄──       Pay Health
        │Employment│           Counseling
        └──────────┘           Redundancy
```

HR Management – First and Fast

"A crisis can emerge in a balance sheet, a union negotiation, or a crook chicken sandwich."

The HR support team specializes in managing the needs of the organization's employees. There are several tools open to members of the HR support team in order to communicate with employees who have been affected by the trauma of crisis. They include:

- Obtaining a full briefing on the facts.

- Assessing what additional HR support is required.

- Establishing the HR support team room and commencing the maintenance of a log.

- Formulating the HR crisis strategy in consultation with the HR member and maintaining contact with the crisis team.

- Briefing the call center on the management of incoming HR calls; such calls should only be processed when the strategy is complete.

- Canvassing employees and emergency contacts to provide them with advice.

- Pursuing information and maintaining updated releasable information.

- Obtaining press releases and maintaining contact with the communications support team.

- Liaising with contractor companies.

- Managing stress within the HR support team and across the organization.

- Providing welfare to employees and nominated emergency contacts or relatives using qualified counselors.

Fighting for Information about Affected People

Human interest rules; be pragmatic and put people first.

The crisis leader is responsible for informing all staff of the organization's strategies for controlling the crisis. With pain comes panic and the management of panic is a question of leadership.

This responsibility may be devolved to the HR member, although the Corporate Affairs member will often assume control of all internal and external communication so as to ensure consistency of updates. Some organizations use staff meetings and an email address or an interactive voice recording designed to reach all employees.

All information provided to the media, relatives and the general public concerning the crisis is controlled by the crisis team, as it is linked to the crisis strategy itself. The HR support team must not breach the protocols governing the release of additional information.

While the crisis leader should relay their strategy as the situation changes, it is the responsibility of the HR support team leader to ensure that their team remains completely updated at all times. The HR support team leader may find they have to vigorously pursue information updates from the crisis team.

With the exception of the HR support team leader, who must be updated regularly, the HR support team should not have access to non-releasable information so as to avoid accidental disclosure.

Crisis HR Rules and the Compassionate Manager

> *People are number one. Families must be told first and fast.*

The HR support team must have access to every employee's nominated emergency contact and next-of-kin details at all times. The team is ultimately responsible for informing the emergency contacts of any employee who is injured, killed, or reported missing. Such details must be maintained in the employee's personal file, regularly updated, and available in soft and hard copy.

During a crisis, the HR support team may release information of a general nature to those callers who have an appropriate need to know. The HR support team must, however, have a clear priority to manage inquires that concern individual employees. Information on the status of an employee should only be provided to that person's emergency contacts.

The HR support team may provide information on the management of the crisis to callers who are not classified as relatives or emergency contacts. Personal information, however, must not be divulged, although queries may be directed to the employee's nominated emergency contact, with the consent of that individual.

The HR support team must remain flexible in case the emergency contacts cannot be located or have not been nominated by the employee. In some circumstances, the nominated emergency contact may be unaware that they have been nominated and may be unwilling to act in this capacity.

Members of the HR support team must be prepared to use discretionary judgment and adapt to meet changing personal and crisis situations. On the rare occasion that personal details have to be divulged to a person who is not the nominated emergency contact, the HR support team must ensure that its reasons are justifiable and compelling.

Under no circumstances, however, should the HR support team act upon casualty names transmitted over the telephone. Confirmation in hard copy, either by hard copy facsimile or email is essential. Most HR support teams will find that carbonized log sheets remain the most reliable means to record information, unless all teams are net-worked in which case an electronic equivalent is best.

In this case, many HR support teams type and talk simultaneously, with the use of headsets. Forms should be clearly printed in block letters and employee notes collected and retained on a single file.

Reporting Individual Status

> *When extricating people from painful situations, leaders handling pain need to make themselves emotionally available.*

Information on the status of employees can be made freely available to telephone responders within the HR support team, or retained by the team leader. This is a particularly stressful environment for the telephone responder, and the retention of distressing information by the HR support team leader acts as a procedural safeguard, preventing the telephone responder's voice betraying the true nature of a situation to a relative who may be unprepared.

The HR support team must remain conscious that, inevitably, bad news travels fast. Therefore, it is vital that emergency contacts be informed by the organization before they hear distressing news from another source.

The HR support team also must ensure that its information is accurate. The backlash from distressed relatives questioning why the organization has not informed them of an accident involving a relative can cause considerable angst within the organizational hierarchy and appear as a particularly unflattering news story.

It is the responsibility of the HR support team to inform emergency contacts at the first possible opportunity that there has been an incident involving a relative.

The team must provide reassurance that this person is well or supply accurate information concerning injuries. An organization that moves proactively in this respect will gain the trust of its employees and, consequently, their extended families. Proactive strategies in managing the contact of relatives will potentially reduce the number of calls, allowing the HR support team to concentrate on those more distressing situations that have resulted from the incident.

In an ideal situation, a senior representative of the organization should personally visit those nominated as emergency contacts so as to inform them that their relative or friend is injured. Limited resources and the geographic dispersion of families may prevent this occurring in a timely fashion. In this case, it is acceptable to call an emergency contact and advice of a relative's injury over the telephone.

Given the exigencies of a crisis situation, it is inevitable that, in some cases, false information will reach relatives. Should this occur, the HR support team must manage the situation with sensitivity, ensuring that if the error is substantial, senior management becomes involved. If the organization is at fault, the HR support team should remain positive and express regret when appropriate.

Reporting Injured, Dead, and Missing

Grave responsibility and the inevitability of emotional pain in organizations.

The extent or type of injuries should not become the subject of discussion between telephone responders and callers. The HR support team should ensure that information, including details of hospitalization, is communicated to the emergency contact as soon as practicable. The HR support team should offer assistance in transporting the injured employee to a hospital.

In some locations, the legal obligation to inform an individual's next of kin of their death may reside with the police force. In this case, it is incumbent on the organization to provide the police with the appropriate information. Either way, the police will usually prefer that a relative, friend, doctor or professional counselor convey this news to the deceased's next of kin.

In this situation, the organization retains its responsibility for ensuring that the emergency contact or next of kin is informed and the HR support team may consider sending a representative either to accompany the police or to visit the next of kin shortly after the police visit. The HR support team must ensure that next of kin are never informed of a relative's death by telephone.

There few exceptions to this are made necessary when the casualty information is in the public domain and the emergency contact is not easily accessible. Telephone responders should note that, in case an employee's local emergency contact calls the organization seeking information prior to a visit, the appropriate action is to confirm the respondent's location and to arrange a visit.

In technical terms, while a doctor must make certification of death, other qualified personnel such as medics can testify to the absence of vital signs. As it could take some hours after a fatality for a person to be legally declared deceased, it is appropriate for the HR support team to act on the declaration of absence of vital signs for the purpose of commencing next of kin notification. The HR support team should inform the emergency contacts of missing persons that there is no information available as yet.

Given the weight of available medical, circumstantial, and other special evidence, the HR support team and members of the organization's senior management may decide that a missing person is, on the balance of probability, more than likely deceased, although the body has not been found.

In such circumstances, the HR support team should arrange a visit to the missing person's emergency contact. The HR support team member conducting the visit should emphasize to the employee's relative that the individual is missing and describe the circumstances as sensitively as possible.

Clearly there are some situations, such as an explosion and fire in a facility known to be occupied at the time, when it may be necessary to advise that the person is missing.

Advising Contractors

Guard against managers becoming "people-eaters".

In situations in which contract personnel have become casualties of a workplace accident, the contractor or their organization will be responsible for informing the contract employee's next of kin, unless an alternative agreement has been reached under the contract.

Should this be the case, it is vital that the HR support team inform the contractors of all steps taken to notify the next of kin. The HR support team should supply any relatives who seek information with contact details for the contractor.

Given the conditions governing some contracts, it may be necessary for the HR support team to manage contractor next of kin using the same procedures applied to employees. HR support team members must be aware of the organization's policy with regard to contractors.

Human Behavior in Crisis Situations

Mass casualty events have double the impact on shareholder value.

Instincts can be our undoing, and research on how the mind processes information suggests that part of the problem is a lack of data. Even when calm our brains require eight to ten seconds to handle each piece of complex information, and the more stress, the slower the process. When bombarded with new information, our brains shift into low gear just as we need to move fast.

We diligently hunt for a shortcut to solve the problem more quickly. If there are not any familiar behaviors available for a given situation, the mind seizes upon the first fix in its library of habits. That neurological process explains in part the urge to stay put in a crisis.

Most people go through their entire lives without a disaster, so the most reasonable reaction when something bad happens is denial.

Disaster researchers call this normalcy bias. When people are told to leave in anticipation of a hurricane or a flood, most of them check with four or more sources—such as family, newscasters, and officials—before deciding what to do. This process of checking in is known as milling, and is common in disasters.

On 9/11 at least 70% of the survivors spoke with other people before trying to leave. If you work or live with a lot of women, your chances of survival may increase since women are quicker to evacuate than are men.

People caught up in the disasters tend to fall into three categories. Some 10–15% remain calm and act quickly and efficiently. Another 15% or less weep, scream, or otherwise hinder the evacuation. Hysteria is usually isolated and quickly snuffed out by the crowd. The vast majority of people do very little being stunned and bewildered.

Around 45% of people shut down; they stop moving or speaking for 30 seconds or even longer when asked to perform unfamiliar, but basic, tasks under pressure. They quit functioning and just sit there. It seems horribly maladaptive that so many people are hard-wired to do nothing in a crisis.

Humans behave much more appropriately when they know what to expect. We know that training, or even mental rehearsal, vastly improves people's responses to disasters.

CHAPTER 7

Preparing, Planning and Practicing

"Prepare for crisis, it is part of business."
– New York Times

Crisis Surveillance

Capability is knowledge-driven and not plan driven. The ability to learn faster than your competitors may be the only sustainable competitive advantage.

Like good strategy, crisis management begins before the first move. Business and joint venture contingency planning for crises is now viewed as both a strategic and operational necessity. Such planning is often described as the cheapest insurance policy to cover an organization's financial and corporate social responsibilities.

The premium for this insurance policy is paid through regular practice, learning from the mistakes of others and subjecting the organization to audit through exercise every one to two years.

Current organizational best practice considers crises as opportunities rather than threats, an approach that makes good business sense on a daily basis. Organizational best practice previously considered "back to the past" thinking to encapsulate its cutting edge approach to crisis management.

This concept has now been overtaken by "back to the future" thinking, as organizations incorporate contingency crisis planning as an integral component of any future management strategy. The crisis champion is the senior manager who influences the organization's culture and budgeted funds.

Organizations seek to implement contingency planning and avoid crises through a combination of:

- Corporate governance
- Risk and issues management, competitor intelligence collection and scenario-based planning
- Business continuity management
- Health, safety, and environmental management
- Security management and threat assessments

The crisis threshold is crossed when these modus operandi cease to be effective in maintaining control.

Conducting Capability Assessments

The seven deadly sins of business are sloth, pride, lust, greed, envy, gluttony and anger.

An organization's crisis capability can be assessed using a range of questioning or training exercises which test for knowledge, skills, and attitudes in regaining control, understanding that capability is knowledge-driven and not plans-driven.

Some of the questions which test an organization's crisis knowledge may include:

- To what extent can the organization detect an emerging crisis through early warning sensors, a system of scanning and issues management, as well as legal and financial audits of threats and liabilities?

- Is the organization familiar with its own corporate history?

- What is the risk of major business interruption within the next 12 months?

- What is the estimated impact of major business interruption and does the organization have contingency plans for such a crisis?

- Describe the crises for which the organization is currently prepared? Which possible triggers have been eliminated?

- What key assumptions have been made as to why the organization should focus on certain possible crises and neglect others?

- Is there a pattern in the preventative actions that have been taken by the organization such as an over-emphasis on technical solutions?

- Are there identifiable gaps in the preventative actions adopted by the organization? What critical vulnerabilities might these gaps expose?

Some of the questions which test an organization's crisis attitude may include:

- Is there an understanding of the crisis system and are responsibilities clear?
- Is crisis leadership included in statements and notions of corporate governance, corporate social responsibility and strategic planning processes?
- Is management open to surprise and criticism?
- Does personal performance reporting include comment on crisis preparedness?
- Is there a critical follow-up within the organization of the lessons learned from past crises and issues? Is the organization comfortable with change?
- Are there systemic differences in the answers to any of these questions across the organization as a whole?

Some of the questions which test an organization's crisis skill may include:

- Is the crisis system supported by a dedicated budget?
- Is there a crisis plan? Would this plan stand up to scrutiny in the event of an internal or public enquiry?
- Are contact lists current? Are the appropriate stakeholders regularly updated on changes to the crisis plan?
- Are the crisis procedures regularly revised?
- Do the existing crisis procedures address the identified risk profile?
- Have the procedures in the crisis plan been tested?
- Are there designated crisis and emergency teams?
- When the crisis and emergency teams were last trained or exercised? Were the teams' responses satisfactory?
- Were the teams' responses measured against a competency standard?

- Is the crisis room well equipped and regularly tested?
- Are there direct silent, unlisted numbers for the crisis room?
- Are there dedicated phone numbers for stakeholders who are key dependencies?
- Are the key executives traditional media trained and social media-savvy?
- In the event of an investigation, can the organization demonstrate that its employees are competent in emergency response as required by legislation?
- Is psychological support available to employees?

The Crisis Plan

Size is not important. Readability is everything.

Crisis plans are useful for inducting new staff into an organization, but other than as the repository of useful telephone numbers, invariably they are never used in the heat of a crisis.

Such solutions are, by their nature, passive. Hence, crisis plans can at best be viewed as a perception of a solution, which, if rigidly adhered to, can stop a team from moving forward in bold creative thought.

Plans are essentially basic or managed systems while knowledge is predictive and exploitive. However, the crisis plan is very useful for staff induction, as it describes:

- Policy on issues, risk, and safety management, with respect to crisis response
- What event or occurrence constitutes a crisis
- What is regarded as an emergency
- Team composition

- Practical actions for the first person to enter the situation room in a crisis
- Individual team member prompts and immediate action guides
- Strategic action checklists for business continuity, reputation and liability issues
- Crisis communications protocols
- Procedures for the call center, communications, and HR support teams
- The stakeholder contact directory

Towards Resilience

> *"I am often asked what single piece of advice I can recommend that would be most helpful to the business community. My answer is simple, but effective BCP that is regularly reviewed and tested."*
>
> *– Eliza Manningham-Buller, Director General of MI5 (the U.K. Security Service)*

Resilience is as much a state of mind as it is documentation. It first involves focusing on people; then, having internal diversity available, and coordinating with external parties. This approach is becoming self-regulating. Resilience is the ability to withstand shock, and it is the blending of management disciplines, described as the "sweet spot" on the golf ball.

This attitudinal approach also leads to sector-wide responses in the marketplace as a continuity strategy. It is the drawbridge, moat, castle and network of castles approach. "Tipping point" is now resilience jargon. It comes from epidemiology and it describes the multiple points of failure, all independent, that a pandemic has across sectors.

Continuity planning is the phased and interactive process, consisting of initially understanding business processes, and then putting continuity strategies in place should outages occur. It is a means to an end, enabling business under threat. Plans are documented advance arrangements often with a "bunker list" approach to aid event leadership.

The discipline has been around for a very long time as just plain ordinary contingency planning. Noah probably had the first formal plan with the Ark and the solution to embark one male and one female of every type of animal. Noah's rule is that predicting rain does not count, but building an ark does.

Business continuity plans often already exist in organizations as unrelated contingency plans and they may be informal or not widely known.

An organization's planning aims to overcome business interruptions which result from the impact of crises on people, property, information, or the environment.

Given the enormous impact of such crises, the development of early warning systems is essential. Such indicators allow the organization to anticipate potential crises, thus enabling the senior management to act to preclude the development of a crisis.

In the event that the organization fails to avert a crisis, effective planning can minimize legal liabilities, reduce the loss of public confidence, or diminish a fall in market share. A well-defined business continuity plan may expedite the recovery of critical business operations.

In an organization in which critical business functions can simply be performed from alternative sites for acceptable periods of time, the crisis team may simply develop and implement business continuity strategy appropriate to the situation.

If critical functions cannot be performed from other locations, it may be necessary for the organization to document its key processes in a business continuity plan by conducting a business impact analysis (BIA). Key processes are those which must be replicated in some manner in case they are physically lost or cease to function.

This loss of process or process functionality may occur as the result of the absence of key personnel, or the loss of crucial corporate experience or assets. Managers who are responsible for documenting key processes must be wary of any organizational fixation with detail that may lead to obsolescent or cumbersome plans.

The BIA is used to formally identify the critical deliverables and enablers in the business, to assess the risks which could lead to business interruption and to evaluate recovery priorities. Once the BIA is complete, it is then possible to determine the range of alternative strategies and options available to mitigate loss and to recover from loss and formulate them in a plan.

> *A plan is like a Swiss Army knife with lots of compact tools in a compact package.*
>
> *In case of emergency, grab it!*

There are many content checklists, such as in the Business Continuity Institute Good Practice Guidelines. At a minimum, business continuity plans must contain the procedures to be followed in response to an outage.

However, it is important to differentiate front-end emergency procedures that focus on evacuations and accounting for people. Business continuity plans are used once employees get to the assembly area and to inform where the business goes from there.

Plans must contain communication instructions for notifying key internal and external stakeholders that the plan is invoked and simple instructions as to where to find alternate sites. It should contain outsourcing agreements with any third party provider.

Clearly, a consistent method of documenting the plan throughout any one organization is useful. Off-site copies of the plan on paper and an external hard drive must be kept by a number of responsible managers.

Code of Practice

- Determine the key business functions or processes, remembering that business continuity planning consists of IT plus everything else.
- Capability equates to a BIA plus plans for buildings, equipment, technology, human resources and workforce continuity, and third parties (BETH3).
- Capability is also doing business under attack or business under stress. Shelfware is just a plan on a table. "Live firing" is sweatware—the ability to endure. Wetware is the ability to think and act under pressure.

Why are plans needed?

Is failing to plan, planning to fail?

The best companies now disclose their crisis and business continuity preparedness in annual reports just as they disclose remuneration, audit compliance, and safety records.

Why is there such focus on continuity planning at present? Quite simply, it is good governance, and it demonstrates current best practice in resilience in terms of having at least thought through what can go wrong at least once.

Like risk, it is all about selecting important problems and fixing them in advance. It is all about asking "What is the most likely thing that could go wrong?" as well as "What is the most damaging thing that could go wrong?" and making professional judgments as to how much resilience you want to put in place in accordance with risk appetite.

Clients expect continuity of service in almost all circumstances. Investors expect management to be fully in control and to be seen to be in control of any crisis-like situation.

Employees and suppliers expect their livelihoods to be protected, and there is a duty of care responsibility. And from an image perspective, reputation may be at risk if an organization does not at least be seen to be doing something.

Code of Practice

- Resilience is the fourth bottom line.
- Capability to respond to widespread environmental impacts from climate change.
- Using the BIA to plan how the Business Interruption insurance might respond.
- Enforcing contractual delivery requirements with suppliers and providers.
- Using the BIA to inform critical infrastructure protection and sector wide recovery strategies.
- Using success and failure stories and disaster videos to get the leadership to check and initiate.

What is involved in planning?

To plan or not to plan; that is the question?

The BIA pulls the critical business processes and their Maximum Acceptable Outages (MAO) together. MAO times should be broken down to subordinate process level where applicable. Key Information Technology applications and other critical assets or single points of failure must be identified for each process.

Since the MAO represents the maximum period of time that an organization can tolerate the loss of capability of a critical business function, this timeframe should be determined by the owners of the critical business function, but healthy peer review is necessary.

The survival or minimum resources required to make these critical business processes work within MAO timeframes are then identified and manual workarounds devised for any gap.

Interdependencies are also identified by breaking down business processes and identifying where linkages exist. The BIA determines non-critical processes that do not require a full plan or any further planning at all. There is often a solid business case for doing nothing.

Indeed, for this reason, planning must be iterative. Do a bit and then check back if it is enough. Do a bit more then check back again if it is enough now.

While there is a heavy emphasis on the BIA process, not all businesses do it this way. Some simply select credible scenarios and plan for them. With professional judgment the outcome is often the same; it just lacks the analytical rigor.

The BIA must be driven from the top down, with senior management endorsement obtained before any detailed subordinate planning takes place. Senior management frequently has far greater tolerances and provides significant freedom action to subordinate parts of organizations. An end-to-end view of the business must also be considered and not just lines of business in isolation.

It is for this reason that planning must be measured every step of the way to prevent futile work. If the BIA is being driven from the bottom up, many people overly rank their relative importance to the value of the business. The reality is that not everything can be recovered simultaneously. Not everyone is that important.

Planning must also extend sideways to third party considerations and not be carried out in isolation. Key external service and material business suppliers should be required to demonstrate that they have adequate plans in place. Often, third-party outages, such as from power and telecommunications, are of the greatest concern.

In an ideal world with unlimited resources, a business would develop a fully-tested and comprehensive plan, whilst at the same time put together carefully chosen, regularly exercised management teams.

However, the reality is that for the vast majority of organizations, planning activities are compromised by limited budgets and insufficient time and resources. Therefore prioritization must take place.

Is it better to try and focus on both the plan and the team or should one area be given the tiger's share of resources to the detriment of the other? The benefits seem to fall on of the side of having a strong team, although some plan development is essential to ensure that the team has the necessary information and that required pre-planned Information Technology arrangements exist.

This is the minimalist plan and optimized team approach, which keeps the plan to the absolutely bare minimum with no complicated procedures and processes, just simple information that the team can use at the basis of taking actions and making decisions.

Code of Practice

- Critical and non-critical business processes
- Maximum Acceptable Outages (MAO)
- Minimum resources and interdependencies
- Back to zero-defect or back to customer facing
- What to do? Minimalist plan and optimized team?
- The BIA is a 'magic formula', but get out of the business continuity cave with an equal focus on third parties
- Employee awareness and education, end-to-end testing and third-party plans

Implementing Capability

The capability belongs to everyone from the Chairman to the Chief Warden.

For the capability to be successfully embedded, resilience cannot be seen to be the responsibility of one particular manager, although many businesses do have a manager to champion the cause. For the capability to be vibrant it must mirror on-going, changing organizational needs of the business.

Too often, fat plans are used as doorstops in offices as they have not kept pace with organizational changes.

Once the leadership has conducted a high level BIAs, the next step is to conduct workshops with working-level representatives from each line of business to flesh out the underpinning processes, survival resources, and interdependencies.

Once there is a completed BIA that truly represents core process and realistic MAO, it then possible to compare this outcome against all contingency plans that may already exist (either documented or just already thought through).

You can then determine what adjustments are required to existing plans and what new contingency plans may be required such as for manual workarounds for any loss of functionality. A plan of action should then be put back to the leadership as to how much further planning is believed necessary. Such decisions should also be sighted by the Board and be briefed to business partners.

Resilience is not to adopt a one-size-fits-all approach, rather diversity and adaptive strategy is the mantra, as there are many variables. In situations where people think that they are more important than they really are and there are too many high priorities, second- and third-party independencies may well influence priorities.

All these independencies can be identified and mapped in advance; less so those multiple points of failure (all interdependent) when tipping points occur in large scale and protracted outages like pandemics. Get out of the insular business continuity cave and think upstream and downstream independencies.

Restart time is another very harsh discriminator. They are scenario-dependent, but they can be estimated with some precision. Scenario based discriminators are another useful tool. This approach has fallen out of favor in dealing with the uncertainties of the future but it remains useful. A small selection of credible and common scenarios may well lead to the prioritization you are seeking.

Most importantly, it is event leadership that counts and while this is not a BIA factor, it should not be eliminated. The BIA is not an end unto itself. It is a tool to get to the default position or start point. It is business issues on the day which are just as important as any advance arrangements put in place through BIA.

> *A BIA is just a document.*
> *Application of the BIA is a leadership function.*

Code of Practice

- Interim operations and full recovery strategies
- Consider doing nothing
- Change travel modes or drive further
- Budge up, displacement or remote working
- Reciprocal arrangements
- Dual site or continuous availability
- The concept of a dead site
- Know who to take the tokens off when invoking home-based IT disaster recovery
- Fortress or geographical diversity
- Subcontracting, warehousing or stockpiling
- Changing the process or ceasing or outsourcing parts of the business
- All risks, business interruption, key man or liability Insurance
- IT component redundancy, site failover and component backup
- Issues and risk management
- Anticipation rather than response
- From crisis management to early warning issues management

Issues Management and Risk Management

Issue management is survival in the 21st Century. Crisis leadership can be described as managing burning issues in a very compressed time frame. The skills required to deal with such issues involving power and passion are no different from those that are used within a normal management scenario, except that they must be applied under pressure in a team setting.

However, Public Relations processes must not dominate the operation of crisis teams, as quick fix solutions in isolation can lead to the escalation, rather than the control, of emerging crises.

- About 40% of crisis situations result from announcements that organizations actually make themselves.
- Around 60% of crises originate with media reports.
- Some 20% of organizations have no warning as the issue breaks and fewer than 40% have more than 24 hours in which to respond.

If organizations have strategic processes in place to manage both risks and issues, they will be well equipped to transition to crisis leadership, as invariably the same stakeholders will be involved.

Senior management within an organization must:

- Anticipate issues and establish priorities:
  Problem + Impact = Issue
- Analyze issues and recommend organizational positions
- Identify groups and opinion leaders who can advance these positions
- Identify desired employee behaviors
- Gain control by using task forces, champions, relationship managers, and checklists
- Implement and monitor the desired employee behavior using lines of persuasion, themes, and symbols
- Select the intensity and timing of media and search for indicators of success

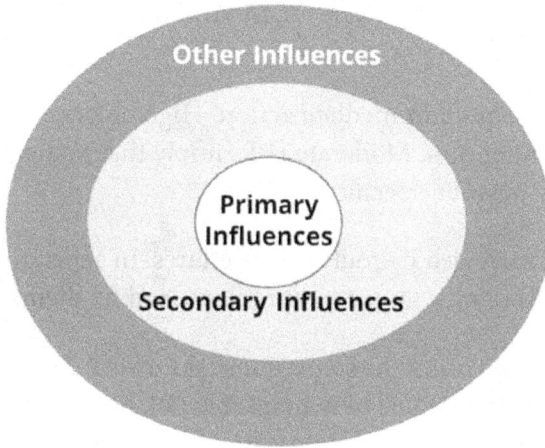

Target audiences

Crisis leadership also can be described as the safety net underpinning risk management. However, in recent years while about 90% of organizations regard the identification, assessment, and management of risks as important, only 50% of organizations outside the finance sector are confident that their organizational risks are being effectively managed on a continuing basis.

Hazard	Insignificant	Minor	Moderate	Major	Catastrophic
Almost Certain	H	H	E	E	E
Likely	M	H	H	E	E
Possible	L	M	M	E	E
Unlikely	L	L	L	H	E
Rare	L	L	L	H	H

"No risk, no champagne." –Old Russian proverb

Extreme risks require immediate action. High risks need senior management attention. Moderate risks imply that management responsibility must be specified.

Low risks are managed by routine procedures. In short, the art of risk management is to pick important problems and fix them.

Furthermore, organizations sometimes take a very clinical approach to assessing the thresholds of manageable risk because the assessment tends to be dominated by insurers and safety practitioners. Many assessments consider risk to be a multiplication of likelihood and effect, but this formula is only useful for quantifying loss or auditing compliance.

Situations that frighten assessors, and those that outrage the public, rarely coincide. Risk from a crisis perspective is a combination of hazard and outrage, and the rules for transitioning to crisis leadership are very clear.

When risk management fails, organizations must deal with the resultant losses before addressing outrage. These organizations must, however, also monitor the public's reaction and address public concerns.

When issues management fails, organizations must immediately concentrate on public outrage.

"Aim to avoid war if possible. If you cannot avoid war, then have a clear strategy to win."

–Sun Tzu

A ship in the harbor is safe, but that is not what ships are for. Understanding probabilities and reducing the impact of unknown events were fundamental to Sun Tzu's thinking.

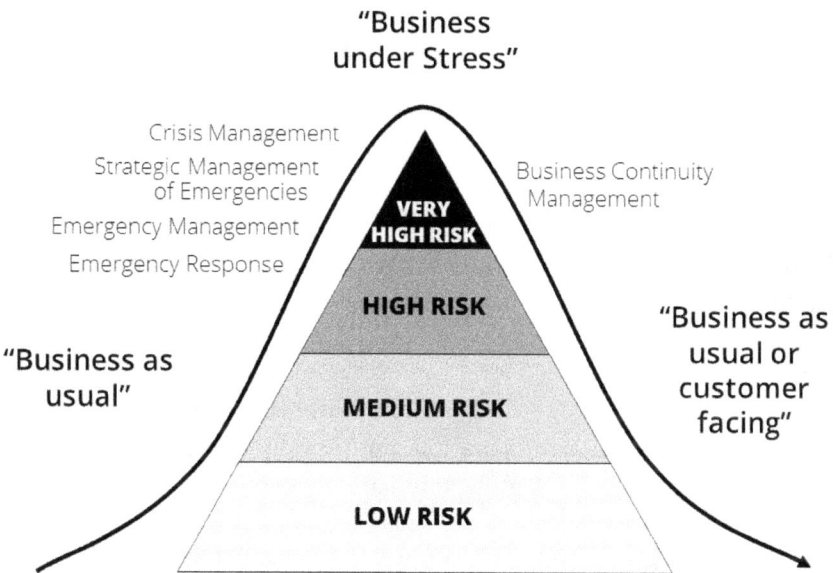

"Business
under Stress"

Crisis Management
Strategic Management
of Emergencies
Emergency Management
Emergency Response

Business Continuity
Management

**VERY
HIGH RISK**

HIGH RISK

"Business as
usual"

MEDIUM RISK

"Business as
usual or
customer
facing"

LOW RISK

Resilience Framework

Resilience = Crisis & Emergency Management + Business Continuity Management

Risk Management

Competitor Intelligence Collection

> *"All the business of war, and indeed all the business of life, is to endeavour to find out what you don't know from what you do, or as he added, guessing at what is on the other side of the hill."*
>
> *–Duke of Wellington*

Business intelligence provides a competitive edge. The gathering and methodical assessment of business intelligence is a critical pre-crisis tool. This assessment can provide indicators or warnings of exposures and entrepreneurial opportunities. The majority of this information resides in the public domain, and harvesting its value is simply a matter of accessing it in a systematic way.

However, business intelligence collection is less a matter of penetrating secrets and more a matter of separating useful information from open legal and ethical source information. Future value must be linked to business taking risks through business intelligence gathering.

The single most significant step an organization can take to increase the value of the information it collects is to increase the speed with which this information is acquired and acted upon. Most employees are not trained, equipped, or organized to collect, process and act upon information.

Conversely, those employees with a contextual understanding of the business situation, are not always empowered to act on information, and would not normally receive intelligence products.

In the collection of business intelligence:

- The information requirement is ideally stated as a yes or no question.

- Indicators and warnings aid the locating of information, whether it be advance knowledge of the launch of a competitive product, notice of an impending hostile takeover, or an emerging Industrial Relations issue.

- "Sources" are defined as the likely repositories of information, whether human, hard copy or electronic.

- Organizations should allocate 30% of effort to human sources, 20% to hard copy and 50% to online services, including imagery, radio, and television broadcasts.

- The reporting format should be specified. Information may be collected in the form of statistics, quantitative value or an actual sample of a product.

- The latest time that this information is of value should be indicated clearly.

Threat Assessments

The secret of walking on water is knowing where the stones are.

Threat assessment methodology is not well understood as it is often confused with risk assessment. Frequency and severity form the language of risk, but threat is measured in terms of intent and capability, and often expressed as means, method, and opportunity. The combination of capability and intent is expressed as high, medium, low, or insignificant.

INTENT	Nil	Limited	Significant	Comprehensive
Stated or known	L	M	H	H
General or suspected	L	L/M	M	H
None suspected	I	L	L/M	M
None confirmed	I	I	L	L

Intent is described as the degree to which the threat source has demonstrated competing roles, adversarial aims, intelligence collection against competitors, or a history of even minimal activity hostile to competitors' interests. The key characteristics of intent are described in terms of:

- Desire: measured in terms of its agenda, activity history, current activities, or merely hostile interests.

- Expectation of success: largely dependent on the source's perception of the threat's ability to overcome the security controls implemented by competitors.

Capability encompasses the adequacy of the threat's structure, size, organization, modus operandi, disposition and finances, and opportunities available. The characteristics of capability are described in terms of:

- Resources: includes its organization, presence and location within its competitors' business sector and market.

- Knowledge: includes not only availability of information, but also its technical and professional modus operandi.

Red and Blue Cell Thinking

Countering a competitor's intelligence gathering is more than risk management.

Top organizations fight for both blue and red information. Blue business information is looking at yourself from a Blue perspective as well as looking at Red. Blue information includes worst-case thinking, some of which may never occur. Red information is looking at yourself from a Red perspective. Red Cell thinking is looking at your organization through the competitor's eyes.

It is one thing to have the marvelous ability to predict rain; it is quite another thing to build the ark in time. The application of Red and Blue Cell thinking gives you edge.

Scenario-based Planning

"Skate to where the puck is going, not where it is."
–Wayne Gretsky. Ice Hockey Legend

Scenarios are the art of strategic conversation. Scenario-based planning can be used as part of both crisis avoidance and overall corporate planning to explore the future in a structured way.

Scenarios:

- Explore trends and provide an understanding of how business may develop in the future.
- Can be used to identify risks, to test business continuity plans, and determine crisis thresholds.

- Are determined by combining possible variables for a series of business drivers. While this is not an exact science, several methods can be used to develop credible future scenarios from a scan of business environments.
- Are traceable paths into the future. As with all scenarios, the stories do not have to be true.

Their purpose is to sensitize strategy formulation to the uncertainties of the future. The value of scenarios lies in their ability to force decision-makers to consider the robustness of their choices in the face of the future's vagaries, rather than seeking the illusion of an optimal decision.

The temptation remains to devise three scenarios such as best case, worst case, and business as usual. Not only are these names unimaginative, they promote the implicit assumption that the future for any organization may improve, may deteriorate or the status quo may prevail.

The key is to have as many, or as few, scenarios as the uncertainties that surround the decision require and to describe them by strikingly memorable names. For any business environment, there are six possible scenarios which generate a complete understanding of possible movements through time:

- good getting better
- good holding
- good getting worse
- bad getting better
- bad holding
- bad getting worse

"Vision without action is a day-dream. Action without vision is a nightmare. The only way to discover the limits of the possible is to venture a little way past them into the impossible."

– Arthur C. Clarke

Crisis Training and Simulations

"Critical action learning I hear and I forget.
I see and I remember. I do and I understand."

–Confucius, Philosopher 551-479 BC

The best plan never survives contact with a risk issue, but simulations can raise issues effectively, expose vulnerabilities, and lay the foundation for resolution. Simulations are primarily intellectual constructs for a purpose expressed through any of a huge number of technologies. It is true that human beings will remember close to 90 per cent of what they experience, as opposed to more like 10% of what others tell them.

Hence, stressful simulations have a powerful, bonding effect on crisis teams when staff is empowered with personally owned experiences. The extreme leadership experience becomes embedded in the corporate knowledge base, and it enables organizations to simultaneously handle risks and seize potential opportunities.

> *"Games are the most elevated form of investigation."*
> *–Albert Einstein*

While there may be many lessons learned from "no-notice" events, crisis exercises achieve maximum value if they are preceded by some form of refresher so that they are viewed by all as being successful, and the experience builds confidence in the organization's ability to control crisis situations. Training also engenders in-depth management, as deputies are often allocated responsibility in excess of their usual range.

Crisis exercises generally last less than half a day and are terminated when the crisis leader is implementing a crisis strategy. One controller observes the crisis team and the second controller directs the counter players. A counter-players' room should be designated close to the crisis room, and each counter player must have access to a dedicated phone or a mobile phone.

Crisis champions should conduct an immediate debriefing of all participants to capture what they have learned from the exercise. This is a most valuable activity, as the best plan never survives contact with a crisis, and the aim is to share acquired corporate experience.

Multi-layered crisis activities with a subordinate emergency dimension are best focused on the activation process and the management of information in crisis, as opposed to the end state of implementing successful business strategy.

If this does not occur, multi-layered, top-down and bottom-up activities will generally become a compromise in value for one or all teams—unless there are multiple counter players to simultaneously test all involved management teams with credible scenario inputs.

With the advent of more sophisticated communications and collaboration technology in the cloud it is possible to exercise in the locations and using the means that would be available during a real crisis. Take advantage of an exercise, not just to learn the best response and behavior but also to stress the technology.

Success is built on a mountain of failure.

CHAPTER 8

Racing to the Future

Will Crisis Leadership Replace Line Management?

> *Business continuity is planning for the inevitable.*
> *Crisis leadership is preparing for the unthinkable.*

The business environment has changed forever with corporate governance, corporate social responsibility and Virtual Crisis Leadership Environments demanding organizations to strive for resilience.

Crisis capabilities have certainly matured across sectors, driven in part by attitudes towards corporate governance. To some organizations, crisis management is still just hot issues management in a hurry. To others crisis management has become corporate emergency response in the aftermath of safety and security incidents.

To still others, crisis management is a subset of business interruption and disaster recovery. Most organizations perceive it as a tool to treat danger and, less so, opportunity.

The reality is that the majority of these philosophies are just planning for what is regarded as inevitable. But what we see evident is that the best organizations also plan for the unthinkable. These are organizations that recognize the difference between crisis management and crisis leadership.

All organizations see crisis management as the tool to regain the status quo or the immediate past. The best organizations now use crisis leadership to exploit the future. They are not so much focused on fixing the hole in the fence as they are of exploiting the opportunities of the open paddock beyond.

Business thrives on instability and there is plenty of room at the top. If you want to have a healthy appetite for risk then you need to have a finely tuned crisis leadership capability to stay at the top.

Some of our clients will invoke their crisis leadership teams, two and three times in one month. It is not recognition of management failure, but rather a mechanism for seizing opportunity and generating business tempo.

This is what is happening in boardrooms and even public sector organizations are rising to the challenge. Crisis leadership may even replace line management as it becomes central to organizational power in an era where information equates to speed.

What is the Point of Acting Conventionally in Business?

Plan – Prepare – Practice – Perform – Prevail – Prosper

The best companies have learned that without business intelligence the formulation of strategy is impossible and that getting inside your competitors decision cycle is all that counts.

These companies understand that business intelligence, simply learning faster than your competitors, provides the only sustainable competitive advantage.

Just as Chief Information Officers are evolving towards Chief Knowledge Officers (managers of the immediate past), so do we predict that Corporate Affairs Managers will evolve towards Chief Intelligence Officers and become managers of the future.

Deter – Detect – Defend – Delay – Dominate

If you wish to lead in business, organizations must be able to function in a non-business as usual environment and to be able to capitalize on negative events. Whether you in-source or out-source support to prepare, plan and practice, best-in-class is benchmarking and learning from others' mistakes and successes.

All executives emerge with cohesion when they participate in extreme leadership sessions and prove that they can align their communications with the operational response. In crises an organization has no friends, only varying degrees of enemies.

> *Always lurking is the competition, whose best interests are served by your nightmare. Circumstances such as these demand leadership.*

Risk – Respond – Resume – Restore – Recover – Review

Leadership is the most important critical success factor in coming out of a crisis. The ability to multitask, prioritize and delegate, remain cool under pressure and comfortable in making tough choices, empathizing, making quick and effective decisions—that is crisis leadership.

Illustration by James Tissot

David slays Goliath with crisis leadership

Appendices

The following are excerpts from the Truscott Crisis Leaders newsletter, Crisis Foresight. We commenced writing these newsletters to ensure that clients are at the center of everything that we do. We are a growth-enabling management consultancy where people are our products.

As thought leaders, our advice is customized to take into account every single aspect of a client's business. This collection of articles is like a modern version of the Pickwick Papers, with widely-ranging topics that generally reflect topical issues at the time of the newsletter.

Table of Contents

APPENDIX 1

Critical Thinking

Crisis teams often have cognitive difficulty in coping with complex arguments under pressure, with the tendency to overlook key considerations because of individual confirmation bias or belief preservation.

The human brain is not wired for cutting to the chase and it needs special tools to check the facts, develop and implement strategy in these situations. Critical thinking in crisis is the ability to conduct three-stage thinking simultaneously and with logical application.

This approach provides the artificial framework for 'cut to the chase' thinking in the absence of physical danger due to the divorced nature of a crisis team room. Individuals may act in an unusual way in the crisis team room because they are suddenly faced with different needs and it affects their continuum of decisional thought.

An understanding of three-stage thinking overcomes Maslow's hierarchy of needs, which effects the psychological, through safety and belonging, to esteem and self-actualization.

First-stage thinking provides for rule-based decisions. It is action or survival thinking used at the very front end of a crisis, akin to the drills performed by emergency response teams who must quickly address the threat, then consider the task and the resources at hand before giving orders in the real sense of the word. It is perception-based retrieval of situationally appropriate responses.

Second-stage thinking leads to choice decisions, as it works through thoughts about consequences by integrating information and drawing inferences. It is subject to the effects of stress as it is no longer a simple recognition-primed process. It is the type of thinking used by emergency managers who must devise a supporting plan to regain the status quo or retrievable past.

Third-stage thinking is about creative problem solving. This is analogous to the thought process of crisis leaders who consider why they would want to follow a particular course of action.

Third-stage critical thinking is most useful when the risk of delay is acceptable, the cost of an error if one acts immediately is high, and the situation is non-routine or problematic and familiar patterns or rules do not fit.

Critical thinking can be developed through training in the use of scenarios to critique and test decision-makers and to allow problem-solvers to consider alternatives.

The best crisis leaders will reduce uncertainty by actively collecting additional information, passively deferring decisions until additional information becomes available, or by filling gaps in factual knowledge through assumption-based reasoning.

Critical thinking follows the sine wave of crisis leadership. If there is too much action, there is a danger of acting too rashly. If there is too much planning, there is a danger of overanalyzing, and thus failing to act. It is all about balance between acting and analyzing.

APPENDIX 2

The Language of Crises

The reality is that the game of business is played in a jungle and not on a playground. Thus the rules of the jungle prevail

Crisis Management has its own lexicon and sets of words.

Crisis Governance	No-fear discussion of the un-discussible; thinking the unthinkable; and accepting that crises are part of business, requiring the convergence of all styles of management.
Crisis Leadership	The rapier-like tool that generates incredible business tempo and which provides a strategic reserve.
Crisis Running	The fluid management of special situations in periods of volatility which may include corporate emergency response, or dealing with slow-burning or creeping issues.
Crisis of Confidence	A media expression probably indicating the incubation of true crises.
Crisis Character	Reputation is something that matters when someone is watching. Character is something that matters all the time, viewed or not. Character is not made in a crisis, it is only exhibited
Crisis Communications	Communications are not what you send out, but what arrives, and the gap exposes a company to media perceptions, investigations and decisions. Ground truthing through contact with media generates speed in the analysis of information.

Crisis Champion	The senior manager who is empowered to influence the company's culture toward proactive Emergency Management and crisis leadership, and the application of budgeted funds for its preparation.
Crisis Leaders	Big-picture, people types who use power, passion and methods to "turn the projector on" in people's minds.
Captainitis	Failure by crisis leaders to seek or consider contrary advice, especially in the business environment where the ability to learn faster than your competitors is the only sustainable competitive advantage.
Crisis Strategy	"The situation as I understand it is this. We see it happening this way." The language of crisis leaders.
Crisis Spokesperson	The human brain works off impressions and not facts. 55% of what a target audience thinks comes from visual (their perception of what they see) and 38% from sounds (what they hear). Adopt a "dressing room" mentality to overcome nervousness, and bridge from questions to "block and score runs."

APPENDIX 3

Corporate Emergency Response

"When the Generals talk you must listen to them."
– Midnight Oil (rock band)

Managing a security crisis can be like going head-to-head with an "Osama bin Ladin" crisis team. Emergency Managers must continue to look at patching the hole in the fence, and their plans and actions must be focused on getting back to the past – solid status quo.

Crisis Leaders, however, must see the open paddocks beyond the fence, and their strategy will focus on getting back to the future and the opportunities that await them.

Special Situation Management

Dealing with Casualties and Improving Communications

Mass casualty plans are now standard as terrorism puts every public gathering place at risk. Responding appropriately in the first 15 minutes is when you will have most impact in saving life. "Scoop and run" is a tactic used by Emergency Services in these situations. Shirtsleeve firefighting are the tactics used by First Responders.

All companies have Employee Assistance Plan (EAP) providers on call, and the best have well developed systems for providing peer support or "fast buddies," like Singapore airlines, which has 200 deployable staff available after any major accident event.

It is now normal to store the list of nominated emergency contacts for all employees in fire proof safes and to have duplicate copies off site. The best companies continually account for all people on site and are able to do immediate name calls and head counts if evacuating facilities.

Invacuations, staying on site with the air conditioning switch off, is equally important as traditional evacuations when dirty bombs are involved. In high-rise buildings, elevators may be the fastest way out, regardless of warnings.

Virtual crisis team meetings are now the norm, as are fully-equipped alternate locations and satellite phones. The best companies leverage technology through Virtual Crisis Leadership Environments, but still use switchboards, internal call centers and hotlines to contact employees in time of crisis.

Megaphones, or loudhailers, are as important as ever, in addition to sirens to directly alert people to serious incidents. A common rendezvous in the event of an emergency is essential as is a community system for lost communications, lost communications procedures for employees and with travelers.

APPENDIX 4

Pre-Emptive Defense: A Business Strategy for the 21st Century

Convergence of management approaches is knowledge-driven and not plans-driven. Having emerged as a strategic tool, crisis and business continuity management has become the driver of analysis, forecasting and management of unidentified and unexpectedly arising events.

The philosophy and methodology is complemented by a reciprocal relationship with risk, PR, law, safety and insurance making its practical applicability a distinctive feature.

That is why Crisis Management and Business Continuity Management are viewed as a central strategy and business tactic.

CM & BCM before convergence takes place	Crisis and BC leadership rolling when management approaches converge	Vision when convergence flies
Basic Management Systems	Predictive Management Systems	Exploitive Management Systems

Crisis and Business Continuity Assurance Statements for Annual Reports

CM-BCM is embedded in our corporate culture.

The value of our converged philosophy has been tested and proved from the Boardroom through back of office and with critical dependencies.

We have practiced our ability to deal with future unknowns; to operate through unstable and unforeseen possibilities.

APPENDIX 5

Problem Plays and Simulated Attacks

Accepting realism and feedback is key to effective preparation for best crisis leadership. In developing the important instinct to act, it is accepted that people behave the way they prepare.

So it is critical to practice problem-solving in a simulated environment incorporating real-time high stress levels.

Military and even sports teams, two groups that live under crisis-like stress, use hostile-intent stories and rehearsals to develop the important instinct to act.

The Outcome of Crisis Leadership

What began as Emergency Management some years ago has developed further through Disaster Recovery into Business Continuity and Crisis Management.

- Crisis Leadership = Crisis Management + Business Continuity

- Mature Business Continuity budget = 1–3% of operating costs + third-party contracts

- Crisis (sector sensitive) threshold = From 5% monthly revenue to 25% of one quarter's income

- Virtual crisis leadership path = Connect + Communicate + Continue in 20 minutes

- Releasable information = Concern + Control + Commitment within 60 minutes

APPENDIX 6
Tips for Great Captains of Chaos

When the Crisis Stalks and Smolders

Understanding probabilities and reducing the impact of unknown events were fundamental to Sun Tzu's thinking. These days, the art of risk management is to pick the important problems and solve them first. The art of crisis leadership is to solve these problems before they arise.

Some may say that business is a commercial form of warfare. Success in business is based on leadership as it is in warfare. Other factors such as information, preparation, organization, communication, motivation and execution also contribute to success but their effectiveness is entirely determined by the quality of leadership.

When Crisis Strikes

Leadership, or the lack thereof, is often the most critical factor underwriting success or failure in managing a crisis. More attitude than aptitude is involved in the ability to:

- Multitask, prioritize and delegate
- Remain cool under pressure
- Make tough choices
- Empathize
- Make quick and effective decisions

Be human. Outside the boardroom, leaders need to make themselves emotionally available when extricating people from painful situations. Be pragmatic and people-first. There is no legal risk in apologizing.

- Be brave. Fear is contagious, but so is courage. Inside the boardroom it takes courage to stand up and speak, but also to sit down and listen.

- Have options. When running from an elephant, running faster than the person next to you is one option but realizing that zig-zagging will stop the elephant dead in his tracks maybe better.

- During a crisis, a leader's responsibilities become infinitely more important.

APPENDIX 7

The Media as a Partner or an Adversary... You Choose

Understand the business of telling people the truth and then you have the choice.

Known to Some:

Each morning PR professionals wake up. They know they must talk fast or be left behind.

Each morning journalists wake up. They know they must get the story first or be left behind.

A crisis is more than just appearing in the news for 3 days in a row. Crisis Management 101 is core business.

Known to Many Others:

In the communication age with 53% of value in companies in intangible assets, you need a large stock of media good will to both survive and prosper.

Crises are complex events requiring a stretched capacity. To look past the zone of horror, seize the first-moving advantage through fast and full analysis and then communicate.

Use a "truth squad" to monitor the media, corroborate and check.

- Use employees as brand ambassadors.
- Be aware that perception is often at variance with the truth. You have to gauge it objectively and manage it effectively.
- "Trust and truth" is the currency of the 21st Century. There is a difference between responsibility and liability.

- There is no legal risk in apologizing, and with media as a partner, it will present major opportunities.

- Good news stays local, but a crisis anywhere is a crisis everywhere. You can expect to be a story every day, everywhere so add Google to your crisis team.

- Print and TV reporters Google to keep up.

- Understand journalists apply a narrow focus of approach to your wide business. In the media world two data points makes a trend. To guide that trend, treat the media as a partner and not an adversary.

APPENDIX 8

Immunizing Your Business

The crisis you have to have

What will be the probable next crisis and the one after that?

Think of these:

	Tick your box
Management buyout turmoil	
The rise and rise of private companies	
Shareholder activism	
e-Biz competitor Botnet attack	
Sexual misconduct	
Carbon trading scandals	
Climate change impact	
More white collar crime and fraudulent reporting	
Energy security breakdown	
Blogs and blast email information overload	
and the others...	

Which amongst these should you practice first?

Or, is there a business case for doing nothing?

Business Continuity Code of Practice – Where's Tiger Woods?

Great; let's get it right, but what's next? How do you stay out in front in this evolving game?

How come Tiger Woods practices in the rain?

Some people say that BC is just silos of people, networks, infrastructure, buildings and applications linked by risk. Others say that BC is doing business under attack. A lot of people say it is getting back to customer-facing solutions. Others now agree with us; it is about resilience.

It is known however that BC alone may not be enough to achieve complete resilience and may even raise false expectations if applied singularly.

Crikey! Some of us have made it to the eighth hole. How far is Tiger Woods in front?

Most people agree that global risks like natural disasters and terrorism are not open to effective recovery by individual businesses alone. Critical infrastructure protection and government-enhanced hardening of single points of failure in business is a key answer.

Tiger Woods said that he attacked himself. What does that mean?

Top companies believe that business cannot afford to harden everything and that BC plans cannot rely on business friends and neighbors; so they conduct threat testing on themselves.

Test yourself. Attack yourself.

APPENDIX 10

What Happens When the Black Swans Arrive?

Sweatware & Wetware – Risk Weapons of First Choice

Is it enough to apply the Incident Command System (ICS) used in some parts of the world for inter-agency cooperation in Emergency Management?

Well, it is enough to at least:

- Manage first response and ensure the other emergency boxes are checked

- Complete bunker lists of tasks and mesh with government Emergency Services

- Ensure organizational security and company assurance

- Run predictable set plays and advance arrangements for particular contingencies which includes most emergencies

But what about when your company finds itself in unknown, scary territory with potentially anxious people in the swamp and no easily apparent exit?

This is the A-grade, high-stakes area when ICS and Emergency Management alone are not enough. Crisis leadership is about the future. Remember in the future it is not the disaster or catastrophe itself. It is how it affected you and what you did about it that will matter most.

You need a system of leadership to forge through the unknown. You need to bring in and apply the risk weapons of first choice to think big, think fast and think ahead. True crises emerge from the unknown. Crisis leadership is dealing with the unthinkable.

- Shelfware is ICS plans in the cupboard, ideal for inductions, contact directories and technical references.

- Sweatware is the physical application of leadership. It is experiential, face-to-face, presence-based, hands-on, applied leadership.

- Wetware is the mental application of leadership; not motivation but true inspiration through advanced problem solving, triggering new thoughts and leadership throughout the organization.

Crisis teams equipped with shelfware, wetware, and sweatware leadership do not pack it in when the black shadow comes across.

APPENDIX 11

Where Do You Want To Be After the Global Financial Crisis?

Strategies to Push Through and Go Beyond

Some companies will harden up and endure, but will not grow. Some companies, through crisis leadership, endure and build a platform to become super competitors after the crisis.

Launch pad: get ready for the known: prepare for the upturn

- Cash is king. Stop financial hemorrhaging through efficiencies.
- Sit on your cash? No! Endure and build. Nuture the best assets, train your people and empower them throughout the company
- Enhance, maintain, and husband your resources; people, assets and existing business. Build an attitude of leadership, not just management, to plan for future growth.
- Promote and build leadership into the front line. Root out any moral hazard and restore reputation.

Leap ahead: go into the unknown, overpower the crisis

- Create opportunities for your market, clients, and partners through building diversity and coordination with new parties.
- Create cash, not by printing it, but through creation of opportunities.
- No vision equals fear. Transform public fear into market confidence and always be ready to go the "Hudson River landing" option.

Built-in resilience leads to competitive advantage

Let the boss sort it out? No way! Companies build management levels and not leadership levels; that is, dependencies and not independencies for fear of loss of control.

Resilience is the ability to withstand shock through the blending of disciplines in the market place.

Resilience is people first, plus diversity available plus coordinating with external parties.

Resilience is as much a state of mind as it is documentation. To get people to dance together, they must have a band and a dance card.

This attitudinal approach leads to sector wide responses in the market place as a continuity strategy. It is a drawbridge, moat, castle, and network of castles approach.

APPENDIX 12

The Business Version of the Eskimo Roll

Paddle your business kayak in any sea – the ultimate in resilience.

The best corporate futures rest not on luck or a "whim of the gods" but on:

- Risk event and hot issue recognition, notification and activation.
- Problem solving and decision making at all levels, on your feet, in leveraged teams, no matter the pressure. Handing off issues to higher leadership to develop and implement strategy.
- Communicating, communicating, communicating as well as rapid return to stakeholder facing.

Accelerate away from chaos towards success

Utilize Virtual Crisis Leadership Environments (VCLE) technology. Anticipate and pre-program the content. Force the increase of the volume and speed of message delivery by overestimating capacity needs. Incorporate multi-channel capabilities and leverage multiple channels like phone, text, email and inbound/outbound mass media publishing techniques.

Empower decision makers to work together. Rapidly enhance capabilities by leveraging virtualization and multi-agency capabilities. Monitor, track and effectively respond to those stakeholders in the communication loops.

Build a reliable infrastructure, integrated with your current technology, and enhance resilience through leveraging emerging resources like Smart Grids across higher speed wired and wireless Internet. Be aware of the traps in social publishing and networking.

The ability to withstand, recover and build from debilitating business shock is achieved by putting people first, utilizing diverse resources, and effectively coordinating with all external parties.

APPENDIX 13

Simulation Stimulation

Be there when the future arrives.

You are going to do simulations anyway, so why not do them the best way? Consider this.

Live participants with plans   Counter-players with complete
and experience   knowledge and opposing experience

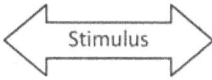

Mind games trigger virtual reality

If you believe it, you will see it. If you think it, it will be. It will work if it is personal. If you do it, you will own it. People learn more efficiently from defeats than victories. Thus, simulations need to push the boundary towards mistakes. Use counter-players to provide that accurate push.

When time and information is limited and the future is unclear, it is disciplined process overlaid by excellent leadership which wins through dangerous opportunity.

Intuitive management is knowing the right answer without knowing the reason why. Crisis leadership is ascertaining the right answer for the right reasons.

How is it done?

Simulations enable people to envision. They "imaginate" your leadership and permeate that leadership down through the company. Simulations in teams are the most effective method to stimulate your leadership to a systemized way of harnessing vision and solving complex problems.

Stick to stimulus

Chance favors the prepared mind; so use simulations to enhance problem solving and decision power for better company plans and strategy.

APPENDIX 14

On Risk – Against the Odds

Does business gamble when dealing with uncertainty?

Dealing with uncertainty informs most corporate activity.

If the perceived risk is too much, companies pull back

If manageable, companies go forward.

When risks are personal and there is more at stake, leadership and systems are necessary to go forward, to push through panic and enable courage.

How do you bet on cash flow?

Risk management is a pre-emptive strike at uncertainty. It enables the taking of risk and it reduces surprise.

Crisis management deals with the rest.

With these tools, risks can be taken, opportunities can be seized.

What are the risk tools of first choice?

The future will be somewhere between the most likely and the most dangerous. Use risk assessments to inform plans and strategy.

What are the tools of last resort when assessments are overwhelmed?

In the absence of confirmed information, assume the worst and use the tools to achieve the best.

Leadership drives everything.

Prepare, plan, and practice.

> *Resilience = (Risk Management + Crisis Management) x Degree of Application*

APPENDIX 15

Crises in the Cloud

IT Disaster Recovery in Heaven or Hell

Heads in the clouds and...

How do you combat crises amongst nearly a trillion instrumented and interconnected devices, objects, processes and people?

The court of public opinion will increasingly live in social networks in the cloud.

There are now over 2 billion Internet users and 30% of the world is online.

What form of anti-crisis planning is needed when more than 800 million people worldwide live their lives, or versions of them, on Facebook?

Is cloud computing sufficiently stable and secure, or will hubs simply become overwhelmed, confused by vaporware, and prone to data theft?

...feet still on the ground

Recognize the cloud as a sovereign information risk in the market-place.

Security, IT, and management must collaborate to maintain situational awareness in the cloud. Adopt an all-team approach to supply chain risk planning and third party crisis execution.

Prevent mission critical data sets from becoming single points of failure (SPOF) or single points of sale (SPOS) by applying industry standards for IT security.

Insist on mutual business continuity clauses in all Service Level Agreements (SLAs) and contracts.

Verify source code escrow for Software as a Service (SaaS).

APPENDIX 16

Want to Capture Learning?
Debrief While it's Hot!

> *I hear and I forget. I see and I remember.*
> *I do and I understand.*
> *– Confucius 551-479 BC*

Why "hot" debriefs?

It is the best way to capture team experience and convert to knowledge that can be acted on.

Is it true that human beings will remember close to 90% of what they experience as opposed to only 10% of what others just tell them? Yes!

Stressful peer team simulations have a powerful, bonding effect on teams by empowering staff with personally owned experiences. They remember how to operate properly.

Hot debriefs, properly executed, will convert this experience to knowledge, and that knowledge to company power. "Armor-up" your company against commercial adversity.

How do you make them happen?

The debrief will fail if the exercise is not properly observed and it is does not include competent counter players.

Do them immediately post-exercise so hot gut feelings are expressed. People speak more transparently after triumphing over difficult situations.

Do them in the very operational room so facilities are a focus. Debrief where you played.

Do them quickly and accurately with a disciplined approach so participants know the activity finishes after the hot debrief.

Do them this way. Controllers give their main observations; counter players give their experiences and perceptions; team participants reflect on their experiences and actions and the C-level leader summarizes and projects into the future

Do them efficiently to capture knowledge, skill and attitudes. Have them delivered in a fast report and go to action.

APPENDIX 17

Physical and Virtual 'War Rooms'

Make it so... Go to action.

Leverage Virtual Crisis Leadership Environments

Control rooms and command posts: "Eyes on, hands on"

- Same time and same place; on-scene commander-centric
- Point to point communications and adaptability to changing situations

EMT rooms "What I want to happen is ..."

- Same time but different place; uncluttered war rooms with practical, efficient communication suites. Wall mounted and projected bunker lists.
- Efficient, common-use, proven, emerging technology

CMT rooms "I see it happening this way...."

- One team to many teams projecting immediate to medium term strategy, think tank culture, brainstorming, and proactive ownership with efficient support groups
- Team of leaders with silent support teams behind each; disciplined but not restrictive structures

Boardrooms "It will be this way...."

- Directing and projecting medium to long term strategy and thinking unforeseen consequences.
- Being creative and utilizing everything to be visionary

The Cloud "Here we are ..."

- Many teams to many teams with global information pull and push
- Meets all places, at all times, all at once with social media on board

APPENDIX 18
Preparing For Business Catastrophe

Do you have a crisis claims strategy?

Anti-Disaster Planning

50% of companies do not survive disasters because they do not have adequate business interruption insurance

Deductibles clauses in policies can make Business Interruption insurance less useful.

Deductibles may be time-based, such as the first-week or a financial amount, and your Business Continuity Plan (BCP) has to cover the gap.

If you have faith in your BCP, you can elect a bigger deductible and only cover extreme events.

Counter-Crisis Execution

You need simple tools to achieve rapid resolution on claims.

Avoid adversarial settlements by using the business impact analysis (BIA) to plan how the Business Interruption insurance might respond and the finance required in the days and weeks following a disaster.

Settlement formula for settlement should be established in advance. Processes and templates for gathering claims data must be in the BCP. These actions lead to swifter settlement. Complex scenarios can take two years.

Include insurance procedures in the BCP to collect claims information and keep the insurer updated.

Testing and improving plans is critical to gaining insurer confidence. The location and accessibility of the BCP is important in assessing likely effectiveness. Savings of up to 15% have been achieved by some organizations from some insurance providers.

Insurance can provide cash flow but crisis and business continuity management are the only way to protect reputation and operations.

Complimentary eBook

Owners of "Dancing With The Tiger"
are entitled to download the electronic
version of the book at no charge
(normally $19.95).

Register to get the eBook at:

www.missionmode.com/free-ebook

Adobe Acrobat® PDF format.
Viewable on most portable devices.

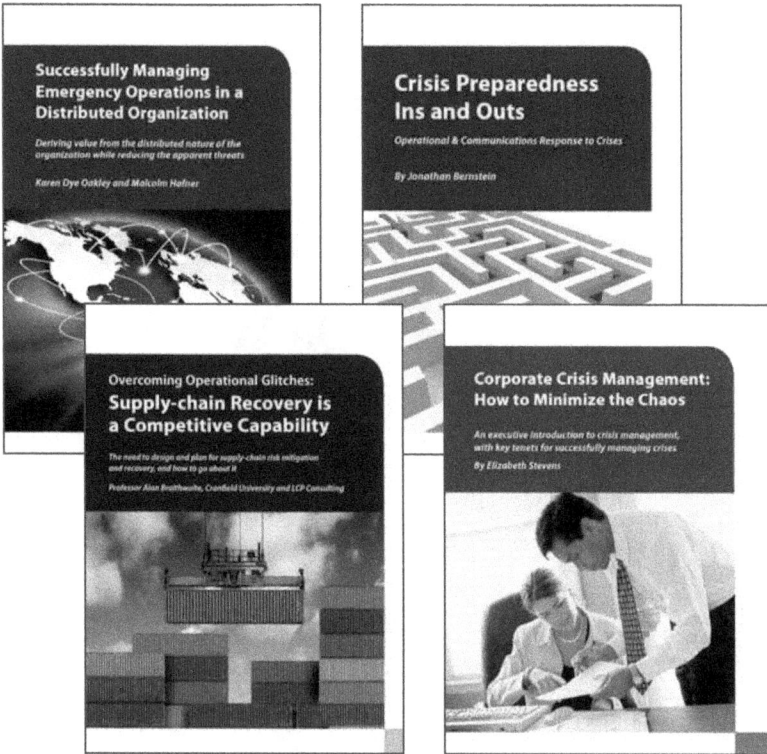

Dancing With
The Tiger

The Art of
Business Crisis Leadership

www.businesscrisisleadership.com

Questions about the book?
Email tigerbook@missionmode.com

www.ingramcontent.com/pod-product-compliance
Lightning Source LLC
Chambersburg PA
CBHW061314220326
41599CB00026B/4878